BACKROADS

——— *of* ———

OHIO

BACKROADS
— of —
OHIO

Your Guide to Ohio's Most Scenic Backroad Adventures

PHOTOGRAPHY BY **Ian Adams**
TEXT BY **Miriam Carey**

Voyageur Press

First published in 2007 by Voyageur Press, an imprint of MBI Publishing Company, Galtier Plaza, Suite 200, 380 Jackson Street, St. Paul, MN 55101-4810 USA

Voyageur Press titles are also available at discounts in bulk quantity for industrial or sales-promotional use. For details write to Special Sales Manager at MBI Publishing Company, Galtier Plaza, Suite 200, 380 Jackson Street, St. Paul, MN 55101-4810 USA.

To find out more about our books, join us online at www.voyageurpress.com.

ISBN-13: 978-0-7603-2772-2
ISBN-10: 0-7603-2772-6

Library of Congress Cataloging-in-Publication Data

Carey, Miriam, 1968-
  Backroads of Ohio : your guide to Ohio's most scenic backroad adventures / text by Miriam Carey ; photography by Ian Adams.
    p. cm. --
  Includes index.
  ISBN-13: 978-0-7603-2772-2 (softbound)
  ISBN-10: 0-7603-2772-6 (softbound)
  1. Ohio--Tours. 2. Scenic byways--Ohio--Guidebooks. 3. Automobile travel--Ohio--Guidebooks. 4. Ohio--Pictorial works. I. Adams, Ian, 1946- II. Title. III. Series.
  F489.3.C37 2007
  977.1'044--dc22
                        2006015955

Edited by Danielle J. Ibister
Designed by Brenda C. Canales
Maps by Mary Firth

Printed in China

ON THE COVER:
An Amish buggy travels past a farm near Farmerstown in Holmes County, in the heart of the world's largest Amish community.

ON THE TITLE PAGES:
A bank barn, with triple ventilators and silo, stands near the entrance to the Piqua Historical Area in Miami County.

INSET ON THE TITLE PAGES:
This bridge, built in 1828 near Middlebourne in Guernsey County, is the only S-bridge remaining that can still be driven over along the seven-hundred-mile National Road.

CONTENTS

INTRODUCTION

FACING PAGE:
*The sixty-foot South Bass Island Lighthouse, near Put-in-Bay in western Lake Erie,
is owned by Ohio State University.*

ABOVE:
*Gently rolling hills make up farm country near Wayne National Forest, north of Marietta in
Washington County.*

Since 1975, when I arrived in Ohio as an immigrant from Great Britain, I've had the pleasure of roaming the length and breadth of the Buckeye State as a photographer, hiker, amateur naturalist, garden aficionado, and history buff. Most of my photographs for more than a dozen coffee-table books have been taken in Ohio, and another half-dozen books on a variety of Buckeye places are current works in progress. Although I've traveled throughout the United States and marveled at the scenic grandeur of the American West, the genteel charm of the Deep South, and the rugged hills and coastlines of New England, I'm constantly drawn back to the familiar, enduring landscapes of my adopted home state of Ohio.

From its 262-mile northern border along the south shore of Lake Erie to its 452-mile southern border along the Ohio River, from the edge of Appalachia in the east to the rolling farmlands along the Indiana state line to the west, Ohio encompasses a patchwork quilt of hills and hollows, rivers, lakes and streams, woodlands and farm fields, villages, towns, and cities. In *Backroads of Ohio*, I've joined forces with travel writer Miriam Carey to invite you to explore twenty-one roads less traveled in the Buckeye State. Although a few areas, such as Cuyahoga Valley National Park and the Cleveland Metroparks, are within a stone's throw of a major city, most of the backroad drives included in this book are well off the beaten track, away from congested urban areas.

More than a million acres of Ohio's woodlands are preserved in the Wayne National Forest and twenty state forests scattered across the Buckeye State, and scores of rare and unusual plants and animals can be found in Ohio's 125 state nature preserves, most of which are managed by the Division of Natural Areas and Preserves, part of Ohio's Department of Natural Resources. Many of these woodlands and wetland nature preserves are located in Ohio's seventy-four state parks, scattered across 164,000 acres in sixty counties. Entrance to Ohio state parks is free of charge, and recreational facilities include nine resort lodges, scores of camping areas, and over a thousand miles of maintained hiking trails. Many of Ohio's most scenic state parks are included as backroad destinations in this book.

Twelve river systems totaling more than seven hundred miles have been designated as Ohio State Scenic Rivers. Most of these waterways are available for canoeing, fishing, nature study, and other recreational activities. Many of the rivers follow heavily forested corridors and offer clean water with thriving aquatic communities. Ohio led the nation in protecting its pristine rivers and streams, establishing a scenic rivers program as early as 1968. Quiet country roads meander alongside some of Ohio's scenic rivers, but many of the most tranquil and beautiful stretches are accessible only by boat, canoe, or kayak.

Holmes County and the surrounding area are home to the world's largest Amish community, and travelers often encounter horse-drawn buggies on narrow country roads. In these gentle, rolling hills, which evoke a scene from a Currier and Ives print, more than forty thousand of Ohio's Plain People

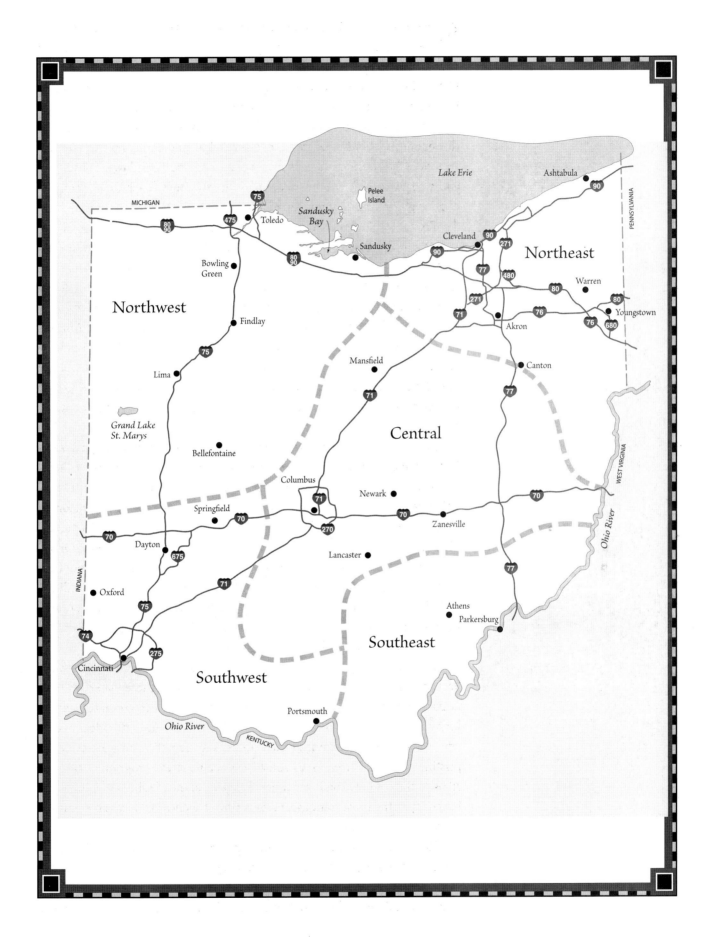

Mist envelops snowy farm fields near West Liberty in Logan County.

Ice covers the base of Cedar Falls in the Hocking Hills. The falls are named, mistakenly, for the tall eastern hemlock trees that grow nearby.

maintain a family-centered, agrarian lifestyle based on strong religious beliefs, traditional horsepower, and self-reliance fostered by hard work, thrift, and a love of the land. Smaller Amish and Mennonite communities can be found in other parts of Ohio, notably in Geauga and Trumbull counties in northeast Ohio, in Adams County near the Ohio River, and in Allen and Hardin counties in northwest Ohio. Each of these communities offer glimpses into our rural heritage, as well as opportunities to savor the delights of hearty Amish cooking at numerous area restaurants. As you travel Ohio's rural byways, you'll encounter historic barns, old gristmills, and more covered bridges than in any state except Pennsylvania.

History buffs are drawn to Ohio's many pioneer settlements, including Hale Farm and Village in Summit County and Zoar Village in Tuscarawas County. The Buckeye State is the birthplace of many famous Americans, including sharpshooter Annie Oakley, astronauts John Glenn and Neil Armstrong, and no less than seven of the nation's presidents. The birthplaces of many of these celebrities are found in the small towns included in this book. Garden lovers will find a wide variety of public gardens and arboretums in the Buckeye State.

Each of the twenty-one drives described in this book can be completed in a day or less, though a week would not do justice to all the attractions that some of the routes offer. The vast tracts of uncharted forest wilderness that greeted Ohio's early pioneers have long since disappeared, but it's still possible to get lost on the backroads of the Buckeye State, so take along a detailed map such as the excellent Delorme's *Ohio Atlas and Gazetteer*, as well as a camera and, for nature enthusiasts, a pair of binoculars and a selection of favorite field guides. Most of the drives are on paved roads, but a few follow unpaved forest and farm roads that may be bumpy and are not always plowed after winter snowfalls. You will never be more than a few miles from a paved road, and overnight accommodations and restaurants are available in every corner of the Buckeye State.

Several of the backroad drives included in this book have attained designation as National Scenic Byways, including the Lake Erie Coastal Trail, the Amish Country Byway, the Ohio River Scenic Byway, and the Covered Bridge Scenic Byway. The Historic National Road, which bisects the Buckeye State for two hundred miles, has been designated an All-American Road.

Ohio is truly part of America's heartland. Although widespread development has changed the face of the Buckeye State forever, the journeys described in *Backroads of Ohio* bring to mind the original chorus to Ohio's official state song, written by Ballard McDonald: "Beautiful Ohio, in dreams again I see, visions of what used to be."

Enjoy your backroad adventures in the Buckeye State.

Ian Adams

Many towns in northeastern Ohio feature homes like this one, the Lew Lawyer residence in Burton. The region was settled by New Englanders who designed traditional town squares and practical homes as they settled into life on the country's then western edge.

PART I

NORTHWEST OHIO
FROM SWAMP TO SUMMERLAND

FACING PAGE:
The Kelley Mansion was built between 1862 and 1867 by Kelleys Island founder Datus Kelley for his son, Addison Kelley.

ABOVE:
Acres of marsh marigolds bloom in early spring at Cedar Bog State Nature Preserve, near Urbana in Champaign County.

Sieur de La Salle was the first European to lay official claim to Ohio, capturing it for France in 1669. He cut a path for expansionists, who explored and settled the Western Reserve in the years that followed, but most settlers avoided the Maumee Valley in the northwestern portion of the state because it was covered with a thick blanket of swampy mud. Taking a cue from the native population, settlers avoided the Great Black Swamp. Mud infected the water supply, mosquitoes carried malaria, and walking or riding a horse through the swamp was nearly impossible. Still, expansion continued, bringing about clashes between the American Indians and the settlers. The Battle of Fallen Timbers, which took place in 1794 just southwest of modern-day Toledo, was a great defeat for American Indian populations. True settlement began when that battle ended. The British were the next group to be ousted from the region during the War of 1812, in a key battle led by Admiral Oliver Hazard Perry at Put-in-Bay.

Amish and Mennonites were the first to take on the seemingly impossible job of draining the swamp. Working through thick clouds of mosquitoes in the murk, they began clearing the swamp and working the land. Construction of a log road through the swamp in the early 1800s made some travel possible—the forty-mile "corduroy" road allowed travel between Fremont and Perrysburg—but only the rugged used it, so the area remained largely undeveloped. Starting in the mid-1800s, two canals, the Wabash and Erie and the Miami and Erie, brought commerce through the region at the fast clip of four miles per hour.

After the Civil War, the shipping industry boomed and ore made its way from the southern United States north to the Great Lakes. Farm goods were first transported via the canals, and later by railroad, to the south. As wealth grew in the Great Lakes region, the shores of Lake Erie became a haven for the upper middle class, and the Lake Erie islands area found a new source of revenue in resorts and leisure activities.

The region is today identified as much by its lush shore life and its small islands as by its quiet farming towns in the flatlands to the south. Defined by a sense of pride, the region maintains natural and historic attractions. Visitors come to see rocks and caves carved by glaciers, as well as the region's rich wetlands and scenic forests. History is important here, too, and a variety of sites tell stories of what the region owes to its politics, wars, and religions; what it gained from industry; and the legacy of wealthy families and enterprising individuals who lived and worked here.

THE NORTHWEST CORNER
HISTORY AND INDUSTRY CONVERGE

The northwest corner of the state was essential to the expansion of the Western Reserve. Its forests were carved up by early pioneers, its swamplands drained, its forts fought over and protected by soldiers against aggressors who came by land and sea. Rugged people settled the land and made it habitable. Entrepreneurs followed, creating canal systems and then railroads

ROUTE 1

Begin in Archbold at Sauder Village and take State Route 66 north, to U.S. Route 20 west, to Goll Woods State Nature Preserve in West Unity, then head south on State Route 191 and follow State Route 34 east to State Route 66 to Defiance. AuGlaize Village is just southwest of town on U.S. Route 24. Follow U.S. 24 east to Grand Rapids. Continue on U.S. 24 heading east to Waterville, then follow State Route 64 across the Maumee River to State Route 65 heading north into Perrysburg.

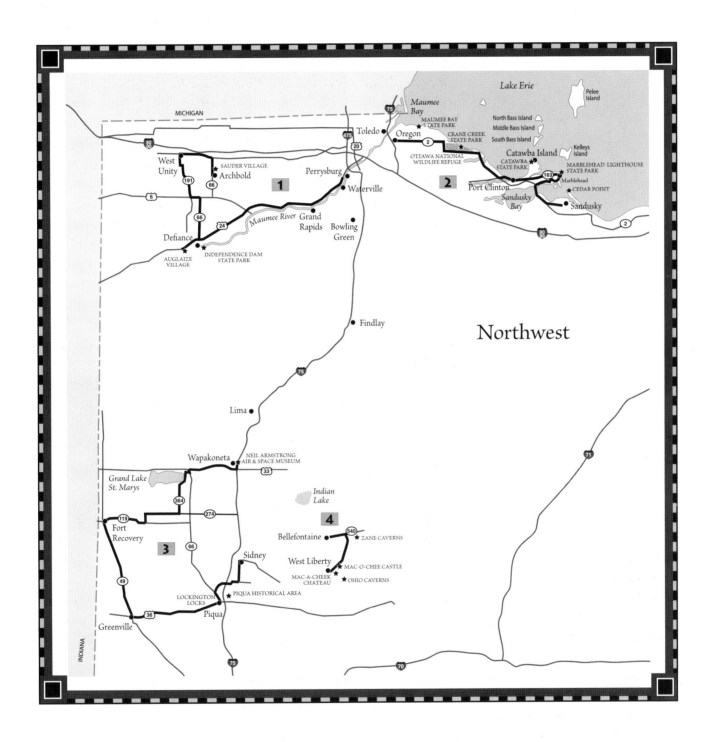

Lake Erie

Pelee
Island

Maumee
Bay

MICHIGAN

Toledo

Oregon

North Bass Island
Middle Bass Island
South Bass Island

Kelleys
Island

MAUMEE BAY
STATE PARK

CRANE CREEK
STATE PARK

Catawba Island

MARBLEHEAD LIGHTHOUSE
STATE PARK

West
Unity

SAUDER VILLAGE

Archbold

Perrysburg

OTTAWA NATIONAL
WILDLIFE REFUGE

CATAWBA
STATE PARK

Marblehead

1

2

Port Clinton

CEDAR POINT

Waterville

Sandusky
Bay

Sandusky

Defiance

Maumee River

Grand
Rapids

Bowling
Green

INDEPENDENCE DAM
STATE PARK

AUGLAIZE
VILLAGE

Findlay

Northwest

Lima

Wapakoneta

NEIL ARMSTRONG
AIR & SPACE MUSEUM

Grand Lake
St. Marys

Indian
Lake

4

Fort
Recovery

Bellefontaine

ZANE CAVERNS

3

Sidney

West Liberty

MAC-O-CHEE CASTLE

MAC-A-CHEEK
CHATEAU

OHIO CAVERNS

LOCKINGTON
LOCKS

PIQUA HISTORICAL AREA

Greenville

Piqua

INDIANA

Goll Woods State Nature Preserve, near Archbold in Fulton County, preserves some of the finest old-growth forest remnants in northwest Ohio, including this large burr oak.

To commemorate Ohio's 2003 bicentennial, barn painter Scott Hagan painted a bicentennial mural on a barn in each of Ohio's eighty-eight counties, including this one in Defiance County near State Route 15.

Major William Campbell and the Ottawa chief Pontiac are at loggerheads during Pontiac's Rebellion, a revolt against the British that gripped Detroit and western Ohio in the mid-1700s.

to transport the region's bounty to a growing country. Their efforts gave rise to tycoons who developed industry, making the region one of the most industrious in the world by the late nineteenth century.

Northwest Ohio's landscape—its natural beauty and resources—suffered as a result of industry's growth. Large tracts of old-growth forest were lost to farmland, rivers and lakes were polluted, and some historic landmarks were lost forever. But people and towns have since rallied to maintain nature preserves and parks, to protect marshlands and waterways, and even to return the skies as much as possible to their original pristine state.

Along the country roads of northwestern Ohio, you can still find early treasures, including barns raised by entire communities, homes built from fieldstones and logs, and small towns with big courthouses. In some places, relics of Ohio's ancient history remain, such as earthworks, ancient burial grounds, and rocks carved by human hands or by glaciers—reminding us of the permanence of the landscape.

Begin a tour of northwest Ohio at the place that tells the story of its beginnings, the village of Archbold. A thirty-minute drive from Toledo, Archbold is a small village, home to about four thousand residents and ten churches. The first church built here, St. Martin's Lutheran Church, stands faithfully on Defiance Street. The town center still looks much as it might have one hundred years ago. Two- and three-story commercial buildings proudly line streets, and bright potted geraniums grace sidewalks in the summertime. A lovely city park features shade trees, tennis courts, and relics from the past.

After clearing the Great Black Swamp and settling in Archbold, residents turned to woodworking, an industry that has proven profitable for the town, supporting generations of Archboldians. Erie Sauder, who founded the successful Sauder Woodworking Company in the 1930s, felt he owed a debt of gratitude to the industry. He built a living history village to pay respect to his forefathers. He collected a series of historic buildings, log cabins, and structures in the region and arranged them together in his own Sauder Village in order to tell the story of what the region was like more than a century ago. Visitors to Sauder Village can explore a tinsmith's shop, a woodworking area, a sweets store, and more than forty other locations in the pedestrian-friendly village, asking questions to costumed docents throughout the village.

Given the woodworking history of Archbold, it's nice to know that only a few miles north of the village is one of the state's most treasured collections of old-growth trees. It's tricky to get to the Goll Woods State Nature Preserve, but the payoff once you arrive is worth it. To get to Goll Woods, drive north on Ohio Route 2 for about 1.5 miles, noting the flat, fertile farmland of the Lake Erie plains. At Township Road F, turn left and travel for about 3 miles, and then take another left onto Township Road 26 to the preserve. This preserve showcases what the settlers had to cut through to create a village and farmland. The preserve is a virtual tree museum, featuring some old-growth oaks that are between two hundred and four hundred years old. Bur oaks, white oaks, and cottonwoods creak in the wind, and a wealth of wildflowers

Five miles of hiking trails showcase the tall trees and abundant spring wildflowers at Goll Woods State Nature Preserve.

Visitors to Lauber's General Store at Sauder Farm and Village, near Archbold in Fulton County, can shop for collectible dolls, McGuffey Readers, favorite candies, and kitchen items.

During the 1970s, Erie Sauder established Sauder Farm and Village by moving dozens of structures, hand-built in the 1800s in northwest Ohio, to their present location near Archbold.

bloom here in the spring. Spring is the best season here, as summer brings the mosquitoes that chased the first settlers from the area and they don't leave until the first chill of autumn.

Composed of one square mile of Ohio soil, the town of West Unity is in the far northwestern corner of the state. The town upholds the Ohio tradition of glassblowing at Glass Pieces, a gallery, shop, and teaching facility dedicated to the art that once fueled a great industry in this region of the country. At Glass Pieces, visitors can tour the facility, learn about the glassblowing process, and even buy some see-through treasures.

The Tiffin River follows a crooked route alongside the road from West Unity to Defiance (south on Ohio Route 191, and then south on Ohio Route 66), where it meets the Maumee River. The route is marked by farmland and offers many opportunities to see deer along the quiet roads. Just east of town, Independence Dam State Park takes advantage of the river and the canal system that used to thrive here. Hikers, runners, and walkers can take to the towpath trail once traveled by mules pulling canal boats, while waterborne adventurers can take advantage of a marina and a nice stretch of river well-suited to waterskiing and boating. Winter visitors, though, seem to get the best sights. The dam keeps the water from freezing, which attracts plenty of waterfowl to the area during the cold months. Swans, geese, and ducks paddle through the water near the dam, while bald eagles soar overhead. Wild turkeys also populate the area in large groups, making this park an excellent spot for bird watching.

AuGlaize Village, about three miles southwest of Defiance, was a project of the Defiance County Historical Society. Like Sauder Village, it paints a historical picture of life in northwest Ohio. Visitors can view early cider presses, lockkeepers' work along the canals, and exhibits detailing how the first telephones worked. Twenty-eight buildings—some newly built and others restored—serve as a backdrop for dedicated volunteers who make crafts and interact with visitors at this living-history museum.

As you leave Defiance and head toward Grand Rapids, be sure to take a slow drive along Ohio Route 424 west, a boulevard that showcases a wide range of architectural styles, including Italianate, Second Empire, Queen Anne, Colonial Revival, Prairie, Craftsman, and Bungalow. This road marks the beginning of the Maumee Valley Scenic Byway, which follows the Maumee River for sixty miles to Interstate 75. As you head toward Lake Erie, the river picks up pace and the roadside boasts notable historical markers—blink and you might miss the birthplace of Pontiac, the Ottawa chief who fought the British, or Chief Blue Jacket's Chair, a chair-shaped rock that honors the brave warrior who fought in this region.

The scenic route passes through Grand Rapids, another canal town that has converted its past into a present-day playland for cyclists, hikers, and walkers. Cyclists particularly enjoy the Maumee Valley views and natural scenery along the riverbank roads and canals. Visitors also come from miles around to enjoy the pleasures of the Kerr House spa, one of a few overnight spa facilities in the region.

At one time, the nearby canal town of Waterville thrived with commerce in the summer and ice skaters in the winter. Skaters would glide over the frozen canal waters from town to town. The town's most treasured building is the Columbian House, built in 1828 as a trading post. Constructed with black-walnut framing timbers (a construction material also used on the building's doors and door frames), it's now considered a priceless treasure. Throughout its history, the Columbian has variously served as a center for society, a local jail, and a restaurant and ballroom; Henry Ford hired the place in 1927 to throw a Halloween bash.

Leave plenty of time to explore the city of Maumee, where the Wolcott House Museum Complex is the historic authority in the valley. Wolcott was a developer in the area, and his wife was the granddaughter of the Miami chief Little Turtle. The Wolcott complex features the family home, a restored log cabin, a farmhouse, and a train depot.

More history waits just a few miles down the road at Fort Meigs State Memorial in Perrysburg. This impressive site is the largest wooden-walled fortification in North America. Originally built in 1813 to defend an imminent attack on Detroit by the British, the fort covers ten acres and contains seven blockhouses.

LAKE ERIE AND THE ISLANDS
BATTLEGROUNDS AND PLAYGROUNDS

Many out-of-staters don't know about the Lake Erie islands—a series of islands that includes Kelleys Island; South Bass, Middle Bass, and North Bass islands; and Pelee Island, which is just north of the Canadian maritime border. Once they know about the islands, though, they become repeat visitors, island-hopping each summer to explore the many pleasures available here. From May through late August, the region between Maumee Bay and Marblehead comes alive with visitors who come to explore the area's geological diversity as well as its highest architectural achievement—the roller coasters at Cedar Point. Summertime visitors are treated to water sports, amusement parks, and cottage life on the beaches and islands. Visitors who arrive during the off-season find fantastic bird-watching opportunities and the chance to mingle with the "townies" in the quiet of the resting months.

Traveling the road from the bay town of Oregon toward the islands is easy. The Lake Erie Coastal Ohio Trail, a national scenic byway, cuts through the area; just follow the signs that take you along Ohio Route 20 for most of the way. If you travel west to east, with the lake on the left and the lake basin to the right, you'll enjoy good views all along the way.

To study the area's diversity, plan a long visit to Maumee Bay State Park and Resort. Situated just east of Toledo along the shore of Lake Erie, this park features marshlands and swamps filled with wildlife ranging from snakes (none are poisonous) and dragonflies to more than three hundred species of birds. Spring brings a host of colorful warblers. Farther from the shoreline, prairies and meadowlands are protected from mower blades, attracting

ROUTE 2

Begin at Maumee Bay State Park in Oregon. Take State Route 2 east to the Ottawa National Wildlife Refuge and Crane Creek State Park. Continue on Route 2 east toward Port Clinton (ferries are available to the Erie Islands from Catawba, Port Clinton, and Sandusky.) From downtown Port Clinton, take East Harbor Road to West Catawba Road to Catawba Island State Park. Continue on Catawba Road to State Route 163 east to Marblehead and the Marblehead Lighthouse. Follow Route 2 east into Sandusky. Cedar Point is unmistakable from the Sandusky skyline—follow the ample signage in town to its front gates.

Limestone boulders litter the shore of Kelleys Island in western Lake Erie.

Some of the buildings in Cleveland and other Midwest cities were constructed from limestone blocks obtained from the East Quarry on Kelleys Island. Today, visitors can hike around the old quarry on a system of trails.

This stone winery, built in the 1870s on Kelleys Island, had a storage capacity of 400,000 gallons. The main building was destroyed by fire in 1876.

23. - PUT-IN-BAY (Ohio). - Fox's Wharf

In the early 1900s, boats and ferries were the mode of travel from congested cities to vacation destinations on the Lake Erie islands. Today, ferries run from the nearby mainland only.

LEISURELY SUMMER DAYS

The little community of Lakeside sometimes gets lost in the hubbub of roller coasters, island-hopping, and attractions in northwest Ohio. Dubbed "the Chautauqua on Lake Erie," this community was founded in 1873 as a restful resort for Christians. This old-fashioned town is gated and cars drive cautiously down streets originally designed for pedestrians only. Cottages here date back to the resort's earliest days, and their spindled porches look tidy and welcoming while the small backyards are muddled with beach towels and blow-up rafts drying in the sunshine.

Throughout the season the town offers recreational opportunities ranging from sailing lessons for the kids to shuffleboard tournaments for the grownups to lectures and family movies in the town's auditorium at night. But mostly, visitors rest and relax, stroll the quaint streets, and sip lemonade on the sprawling front porch of Hotel Lakeside, which dates back to 1875.

For a gate fee, passersby can visit Lakeside for a day, or even for an hour, to take in the antique feel of the village and enjoy a walk along the lake. To stay the week, book a cottage.

prairie critters, which probably are a thorn in the side of the groundskeeper in charge of the resort's nearby eighteen-hole golf course. The resort features a lodge, cottages, and campgrounds, meeting the needs of those who crave anything from an upscale to a truly rural experience.

Birders often converge on Ottawa National Wildlife Refuge, a system made up of three areas: Cedar Point National Wildlife Refuge, Ottawa National Wildlife Refuge, and West Sister Island National Wildlife Refuge. In the fall, almost 70 percent of the Mississippi Flyway population land in the area, seeking food and lodging and attracting a host of visitors loaded with binoculars, cameras, and field guides. Even novice bird-watchers appreciate the theater of wilderness created at this center of natural beauty.

Though it is part of the park system, visitors aren't allowed on West Sister Island. This eighty-three-acre island provides a great habitat for birds and wildlife, but the ground is covered with poison ivy. Boaters, however, can get close enough to the island to get a look at the spectacle of winged creatures through a set of spyglasses, so die-hard birders are encouraged to rent a boat at one of the area's many marinas for an afternoon of prime bird watching from a distance.

Birders also like to visit nearby Crane Creek State Park, where bald eagles and other raptors are spotted often; an observation deck provides additional viewpoints to avian fans. Sun worshipers can relax on the park's 3,500-foot sandy beach.

From Ottawa National Refuge, head east to Port Clinton, the "walleye capital of the world." Lake Erie is the southernmost and shallowest of the Great Lakes, features that encourage a large fish population. The annual catch from Lake Erie often equals the combined catch from the other four Great Lakes. But visitors beware: the shallow waters, particularly in this portion of the lake, can get violently dangerous when storms creep up. Be sure to check the weather before renting a boat for the day.

Things nautical set the theme in Port Clinton. Restaurants in this historic town range from fantastic greasy spoons where the walleye is fried fresh, to charming, old-fashioned eateries like the legendary Garden Restaurant, which serves upscale American cuisine. Shops and attractions give visitors a reason to stay on the mainland, while three ferry companies provide access to nearby islands.

On sunny summer days, the sky pulls a blue sheen out of Lake Erie, and the contrast of the blue sky with the green lawns and trees along the shoreline is stunning. It is particularly delightful to observe this scene on the drive from Port Clinton to Catawba Island. Drive slowly—the cottages and vacation homes along the road are the summer locale for families with young kids, who paddle across the street in beach sandals, struggling to carry rafts and sand buckets. The scene can sometimes seem so Rockwellian, it's hard to believe you're in the twenty-first century.

Catawba Island is attached to the mainland by a causeway and is home to Catawba Island State Park, a small park that serves as the "mainland" headquarters for state parks on the nearby islands. Visitors can also hop on

This brightly painted house is located east of Put-in-Bay on South Bass Island.

During severe winters, ice formations form along the limestone cliffs on South Bass Island.

Fishing shanties dot the ice between Put-in-Bay and Gibraltar Island on western Lake Erie. Favorable winter conditions produce large catches of perch and walleye for winter anglers.

car and passenger ferries from Catawba Point for trips to Put-in-Bay and to Middle Bass Island.

Kelleys Island, at four square miles, is the largest of the Lake Erie islands. In addition to beautiful landscapes and six miles of hiking trails, the island has two unique features. Inscription Rock gives testimony to American Indians who lived here more than five hundred years ago; their pictographic writings are carved in limestone and remain a curiosity today. Even older are the island's glacial grooves, a flowing series of furrows carved into the rock some 400 million years ago. Measuring 400 feet long, 35 feet wide, and 10 feet deep, the grooves are home to ancient marine fossils; take a tour to get the full details about this groovy geological site.

Lake Erie Island life seems to present two options: explore or party. Visitors to South Bass Island's Put-in-Bay area typically have partying in mind, and the town's bars, nightclubs, and restaurants are ready to accommodate bachelors' parties, groups of recent college grads, and old-timers hoping to recapture their glory days. Avoid the bay on nights and weekends if your aim is a quiet experience.

In addition to housing revelers, South Bass Island pays homage to a rebel. Oliver Hazard Perry defeated the British here during the War of 1812, securing Lake Erie and coining the phrase "We have met the enemy and they are ours." Today, the Perry's Victory and International Peace Memorial monument towers 352 feet into the sky. Visitors can take an elevator to the open-air rotunda for a fantastic view of the islands and the mainland.

Middle Bass Island also maintains its own character. Since their earliest settlement, the islands have enjoyed a reputation as a good habitat for vineyards—the soil is rich and the lake fosters late-season frosts. In the mid-1800s, wines produced here rivaled the best in Europe. On Middle Bass Island, the Lonz family emerged as the leading vintner of the islands, growing grapes and producing wines. They even survived Prohibition by bottling grape juice with a label that sported "how to ferment wine" instructions. The winery was a hot spot for tourism until the structure's terrace collapsed in 2000, a tragedy that killed one person and injured more than seventy-five. The state of Ohio purchased the winery and more than 120 acres of land on the island and is currently converting the land into a state park.

When you return to the mainland, head east toward Marblehead for a view of Marblehead Lighthouse State Park. This popular lighthouse is open for tours on select summer afternoons from Memorial Day to the Friday before Labor Day. It requires some old-fashioned climbing, but the climb yields a lighthouse keeper's view of the mainland and islands, with all the mystique and charm an old lighthouse can deliver.

From Marblehead, it's a short drive to Sandusky, home of Cedar Point, one of the nation's most beloved amusement parks. From its storied Blue Streak—the oldest coaster in the park—to the new Top Thrill Dragster, a behemoth that reaches speeds of 120 miles per hour and heights of 420 feet, the park maintains its reputation as a world leader in the coaster game, housing seventeen of the world's most famous thrill rides.

LAND OF TALL CHURCHES
THE FRONTIER OF THE OLD WEST
AND THE GATEWAY TO THE NEW FRONTIER

With a history steeped in the battle between European Christianity, American Indian traditions, and American politics, the Land of Tall Churches, the portion of the state between Cincinnati and Toledo, has given the world its share of heroes. The great chieftains converged here—Blue Jacket, Tecumseh, the Prophet, Little Turtle, and others—to try to forge a future for their people. Europeans settled the land and tamed its forests; Annie Oakley hunted in the region's nooks and glens; and a young boy gazed at the moon, not knowing that one day he'd be the first to walk on its surface.

Years before Neil Armstrong grew up in Wapakoneta, the great chieftains met here. They built a council house at Wapakoneta and accepted arms from the British to fight against the encroachment on their land by settlers. The Treaty of Greenville in 1795 signaled the beginning of the end for the tribes, and they headed west in search of new land, leaving Wapakoneta behind to be settled by the white men. The settlers who followed built homes, churches, and schools in the architectural style that they remembered from their homeland—buildings with tall spires that reached to the sky. In 1979, more than fifty buildings in the region were placed on the National Register of Historic Places, making this area significant for both its history and its architecture.

But Neil Armstrong put the city on the modern map. His achievements are celebrated at the Neil Armstrong Air and Space Museum, a facility proudly dedicated in 1972 to the town's local hero. The museum houses the original Gemini VIII spacecraft, and it continues to add new exhibits to its repertoire of space paraphernalia—most recently a space-shuttle landing simulator and a lunar landing simulator.

Head west out of town on Ohio Route 33 to St. Marys. Though much of this region was once forested, the trees were felled to create farmland, and fields of corn and soybeans now grow here. The most distinguishing feature of St. Marys is its namesake, Grand Lake St. Marys. Once the largest man-made lake in the world, it was originally created over a wet prairie as a reserve for the regional canal system. It now functions as a happy landing for migrating birds, as a hatchery for the state's fish population, and as a state park to be enjoyed by anyone who makes the drive to its shores. The town celebrates its canal history at St. Marys Memorial Park, with the Belle of St. Marys, a full-scale replica of a canal boat.

Two lighthouses adorn the shores of Grand Lake St. Marys. The Northwood Lighthouse no longer works, but it can be seen by boaters floating

ROUTE 3

Begin at the Neil Armstrong Museum just west of Interstate 75 at exit 111 in Wapakoneta. Take I-75 south to the next exit, U.S. Route 33 heading west to U.S. Route 66 heading south, then follow State Route 703 west to Grand Lake St. Marys. Follow State Route 364 south to State Route 274 west to U.S. Route 127 south to State Route 119 west to Ft. Recovery. From Ft. Recovery, follow State Route 49 south to Greenville, then take State Route 571 east to State Route 36 east into Piqua and follow State Route 66 north to North Hardin Road and follow the signs to the Piqua Historical Area State Memorial and the Lockington Locks. Continue on North Hardin Road, (County Road 110) to County Road 111 east. Turn right on the Miami-Conservancy Road and take a quick left onto East Lockington Road north. Follow East Lockington to Miami River Road north into Sydney.

The army of General "Mad" Anthony Wayne constructed the four-blockhouse post at Fort Recovery near the Indiana border in March 1794. Later that year, Wayne won the pivotal Battle of Fallen Timbers in northwest Ohio against a large American Indian force.

BELOW: *A dairy barn shelters Holsteins near Carthagena in rural Mercer County.*

The main building of Saint Augustine Catholic Church at Minster, in Mercer County, was built in the neoclassical style in 1848. The twin spires were added in 1874.

AUTUMN LEAF-PEEPING

About 33 percent of Ohio is forested, and two areas of the state—the southeastern portion, particularly in Wayne National Forest, and the Mansfield area—are noteworthy when the leaves start to turn. Near Mansfield, Mohican State Park and Forest provides all the trappings of the season. Canoes are available for hire along the Mohican River; scenic, curvaceous drives are best taken in a convertible; and hikers of every sort can enjoy the views and vistas throughout the park. But one of the most unusual spots available to the fearless is the Mohican Fire Tower. Once a part of a large system of fire towers throughout the region, the tower was lovingly restored in 2005 and now serves as a lookout point for curious visitors. Climbers are rewarded with stunning views in every direction, particularly on crisp autumn days. The climb is connected to a series of hiking trails that range from easy to difficult, in and around the Mohican State Park system.

Chief Sitting Bull called five-foot-tall Annie Oakley "Little Sure Shot." Born near Greenville in 1860, Annie here poses for the camera around 1899. The star of Buffalo Bill's Wild West Show, Annie's marksmanship was celebrated throughout the United States and Europe.

on the northern section of the lake. The Rotary Lighthouse, constructed in 1986, features an observation deck.

Farther west and a sharp turn south, Fort Recovery State Museum memorializes two battles from the Indian wars. Exhibits at the authentically restored fort tell the story of the defeat of General St. Clair in 1791, as well as the story of the success of General "Mad" Anthony Wayne three years later. Fort Recovery Monument Park honors the men who fought here under the generals.

Head south toward Greenville, and you'd better get your gun. Perhaps it was the city's amazing history that inspired Annie Oakley. It was here that Mad Anthony established Fort Greene Ville, and where the Treaty of Greenville was signed in 1795, opening up the Western Territory for expansion. Driving along the country road that leads into town, you can easily imagine a young Annie Oakley practicing her shot and hunting rabbits for her family's dinner. Eight parks and preserves ring the city, representing wetlands, woodlands, prairies, and historical sites.

The little town of Greenville proudly touts its place in history while maintaining a vibrant sense of small-town bigness. It also maintains a healthy pride in its present and future. KitchenAid is one of the city's best corporate citizens; this manufacturer of kitchen appliances houses an interesting museum-meets-store in the downtown district.

Farther east toward Piqua, the Piqua Historical Area State Memorial offers a picturesque and unique view of the area's history. Located in the home of John Johnston, a U.S. Indian Agent who served from 1812 to 1829, this living history museum gives visitors a firsthand view of what life was like for the prosperous of the time. Johnston's homestead includes the family home, a summerhouse, a cider press, and one of the oldest, largest barns in the state. Throughout the property, various points of interest represent a convergence of the history of the area. From mysterious mounds constructed by the Adenas (an ancient culture that lived in the region more than two thousand years ago), to the canal that passes by the property, to the slice of history represented by Johnston's home, visitors to the Piqua memorial truly witness a slice of Ohio history.

Five miles north of Piqua, the Lockington locks and dam represent some of the best engineering along the Ohio and Erie Canal system. Well-preserved, the structures shouldn't be missed as you travel the road to Sidney.

Downtown Sidney, with its many historic and significant buildings, is a National Registered Historic District. Sidney's downtown courthouse square features architecture ranging from the Monumental Building, a post–Civil War structure that was constructed to honor the war's dead; to the Shelby County Courthouse, named a Great American Public Place; to the Peoples Savings and Loan building, designed by architect Louis Sullivan and opened in 1918. Walk through Shelby and observe its treasure of American architecture, and then take a drive to the town's Tawawa Park to see one of Shelby's simplest but most elegant structures, the Sidney Covered Bridge.

A group of showy lady's slipper orchids blooms in late spring at Cedar Bog State Nature Preserve near Urbana in Champaign County.

Ohio Caverns, east of West Liberty in Logan County, are the largest caverns open to the public in the Buckeye State.

Castle Piatt Mac-O-Chee, completed by Colonel Donn Piatt in 1881, is one of two castles built by the Piatt brothers a few miles east of West Liberty. Donn's brother Abram Sanders Piatt built the other, called Castle Piatt Mac-A-Cheek.

ROUTE 4

Begin in downtown Bellefontaine at the Orr Mansion on Columbus Avenue. Take State Route 540 east to the Hi-Point Career Center's Campbell Hill, and follow Route 540 east to Zane Caverns. From there, take County Road 5 south to State Route 245 east to find the Ohio Caverns. Head west on Route 245 to Township Road 47—Mac-A-Cheek Castle is on your right, and the staff will provide directions to Mac-O-Chee Castle and the original log house from there.

Begin a road trip in this region by taking your foot off the brake at the beginning of Bellefontaine's McKinley Street—tap the brakes within a few seconds and you've driven down the world's shortest street. It's only seventeen feet long. While downtown, be sure to take a look at the town's favorite outdoor exhibit, the first concrete street in America. Poured and set in 1801, this slab paved the way for modern American roads in this town, which ironically made its mark by courting the railroad lines.

It's hard to miss the Logan County Courthouse in downtown Bellefontaine. The Franco-Italian architecture is austere; if it weren't so wonderfully kept up, it would look like a haunted house on a movie lot. But the best way to see the town is to drive a few minutes outside of town to Campbell Hill, the highest point in Ohio. Rising 1,549 feet above sea level, the hill serves as the inspirational site for the Ohio Hi-Point Career Center. Look for the marker in the center's parking lot.

Logan County had its share of railroad and lumber barons during the nineteenth and early twentieth centuries; these barons left their marks on the

Mac-O-Chee Castle peeks out from the trees in West Liberty at the beginning of the twentieth century; the picture remains much the same at the beginning of the twenty-first century.

area in the form of mansions and castles. In Bellefontaine, the Orr Mansion is preserved by the local historical society. A tour of the home provides a glimpse into the lives of the rich and famous more than a hundred years ago, and the historical society's museum portrays an accurate picture of life in the Logan County area before and after European settlement.

Just east of town, almost to Zanesville, exploration descends underground at Zane Caverns. The two-level caves are open for tours and provide a glimpse into a rare geological phenomenon called cave pearl formations—rock that has been molded into pearl-like stones. Operated by the Shawnee Remnant Band, the property also houses the Shawnee and Woodland Native American Museum.

Spelunkers should head south toward West Liberty for a tour of the Ohio Caverns, the state's largest caverns. Housed in a "museum" that maintains a constant temperature of 54 degrees Fahrenheit, the Ohio Caverns are a welcome diversion on a hot, muggy summer day. Bring a picnic, as the site's thirty-five-acre park above the stalactites is a truly lovely spot.

Those who go below ground to view the caverns will find pristine white stalactites and colorful, diverse formations. But these colorful caverns are not for the faint of heart. The mile-long tour takes forty-five minutes to complete, and tall visitors will have to do a bit of stooping. If you're claustrophobic, you might want to stay aboveground and look at photos in the visitor center instead.

Logan County's diverse geography—from underground caves to distinctly aboveground rivers—makes a drive through its countryside a pleasure. It's quiet here, and pristine. Ambling through West Liberty, it's easy to imagine a judge from Cincinnati choosing to relocate his family here. That's what Judge Piatt did in the 1820s. The log cabin that the judge originally occupied is now known as the Pioneer House, and though it's now an antique shop, it shows the humble beginnings even a successful judge endured in early Ohio. Judge Piatt persevered, and the success of his family is marked by the Piatt Castles, a source of pride for locals and of curiosity for visitors. The two stone castle-like homes—named Mac-A-Cheek and Mac-O-Chee—signaled prosperity for the family. It is where abolitionists, poets, men (and women) of commerce, and newspapermen met to discuss the issues of the day. The Piatts' connection to West Liberty hasn't dissipated since the judge laid the first log for his cabin. The castle tour celebrates the family spirit, shows the respect the Piatts had for the nature of the area and for the American Indians who lived nearby, and reveals a great deal about the politics of the region throughout the family's two-hundred-year history. Tours have been given here ever since the homes were first opened to the public in the 1920s. Margaret Piatt still works hard to maintain the property and the foundation that supports it.

PART II

NORTHEAST OHIO
NEW ENGLAND'S WESTERN EDGE

FACING PAGE:
The forty-two-foot Fairport Harbor West Breakwater Lighthouse, with its attached keeper's house, was completed in June 1925. It is still in active use today.

ABOVE:
Each year in midsummer, more than four hundred participants stage a Civil War encampment and battle at Hale Farm and Village in Cuyahoga Valley National Park.

Northeast Ohio once represented the edge of the Western Reserve. Many of the state's earliest settlers arrived here from Connecticut, giving the region a decidedly Eastern flair, and relics of the early settlers—particularly the area's many covered bridges in the northern part of the region—are charming reminders of our forefathers' craftsmanship. Just south of Cleveland, the region's rich farmland supports the largest Amish and Mennonite community in the world, providing yet another glimpse into what the Western Reserve was like before the emergence of the Rust Belt.

Industry is celebrated here, too, and often collides with nature. The ruins of a paper mill in Cuyahoga Valley National Park give hikers pause, and south of the park, in Akron, the canal runs right into the city, near the National Inventors Hall of Fame and Museum. Thomas Edison's birthplace, about forty miles west of Cleveland, marks another industrial genius, while the nation's first streetlamp still lights Cleveland's Public Square. And visitors to Youngstown and Warren can't help but notice the impact that industry has had on the area: smokestacks and train tracks still give shape to the landscape and skyline.

But the region's best quality is its love for—and preservation of—its natural landscape. Gorges, valleys, and hills are celebrated in parklands, some of which were donated by industrialists with names like Rockefeller. If Cleveland's Metroparks system creates an "emerald necklace" around the town, Cuyahoga Valley National Park, stretching from the southern edge of Cleveland to Akron, could be considered the necklace's dangling jewels. Farther south, the Mohican State Forest and state park system celebrate the rich, river-streaked land.

In a single day's drive, it's possible to experience the sandy shores of Lake Erie, the hilly heights of a forest ridge, an urban center, a covered wooden bridge, a swing bridge, and countryside dotted with barns constructed more than two hundred years ago that will never know the intrusion of an electric light bulb. That's diversity.

THE LAKE ERIE SHORELINE
CLIFFS AND BEACHES

Ohio is home to seven presidents. Their histories are celebrated throughout the state, but President Garfield arguably enjoys the most notable honors of all his Ohio-born presidential brothers. In Cleveland's Lake View Cemetery, the Garfield Memorial is a must-see. An imposing stone memorial that stands 180 feet high, this walk-through monument features all the gilding available in the late 1800s, suitable for a president assassinated in office—stained glass windows, winding marble staircases, and bronze caskets of Garfield and his wife, Lucretia, indoors with observation porches overlooking the cemetery and affording a view of Lake Erie on a clear day.

Garfield's life is celebrated at the James A. Garfield National Historic Site just east of Cleveland in Mentor, where this tour begins. A sprawling home with a large front porch was the site of the president's "front porch campaign."

ROUTE 5

Begin at Lake View Cemetery in Cleveland and take U.S. Route 20/6 east to Interstate 90/State Route 2 east. Continue on Route 2 east to the Mentor Avenue exit, then head east to the James Garfield National Historic Site. Follow Route 306 south to Kirtland. Then return to Route 306, heading north back to Route 2 east. Take the Richmond Street exit toward Fairport Harbor Lakefront Park and Mentor Headlands, and follow Route 2 east past Madison and into Geneva-on-the-Lake, then follow State Route 531 east into Ashtabula.

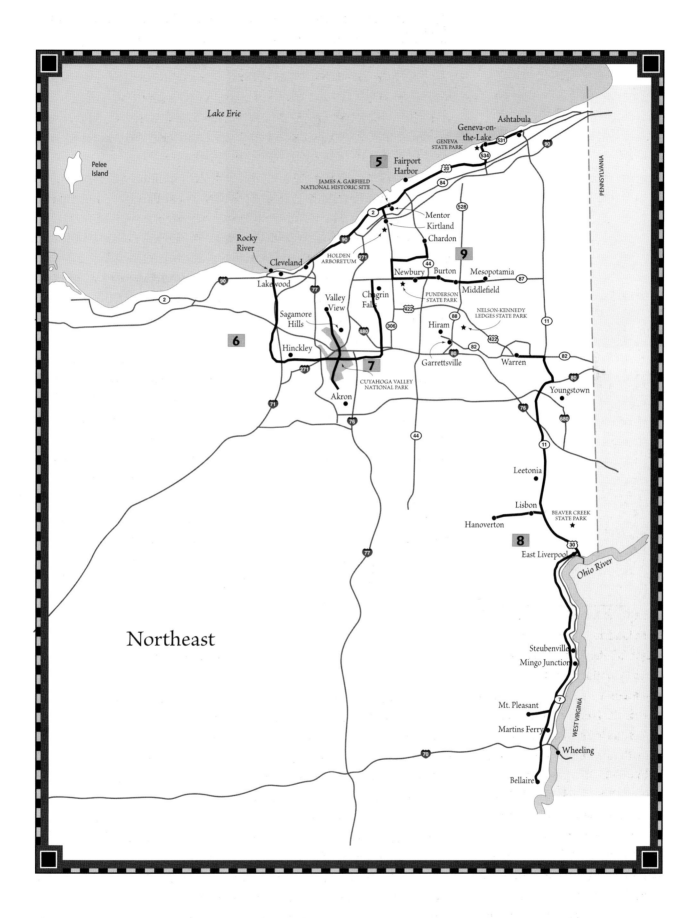

Lake Erie

Pelee
Island

Ashtabula

Geneva-on-
the-Lake

GENEVA
STATE PARK

5 Fairport
Harbor

JAMES A. GARFIELD
NATIONAL HISTORIC SITE

Mentor
Kirtland
Chardon

PENNSYLVANIA

Rocky
River

Cleveland

Lakewood

HOLDEN
ARBORETUM

9

Newbury Burton Mesopotamia

Middlefield

Valley
View

Chagrin
Falls

PUNDERSON
STATE PARK

NELSON-KENNEDY
LEDGES STATE PARK

Sagamore
Hills

6

Hinckley

Hiram

Garrettsville Warren

7

CUYAHOGA VALLEY
NATIONAL PARK

Akron

Youngstown

Leetonia

Lisbon

Hanoverton

BEAVER CREEK
STATE PARK

8

East Liverpool

Ohio River

Steubenville

Mingo Junction

Mt. Pleasant

WEST VIRGINIA

Martins Ferry

Wheeling

Bellaire

Northeast

Holden Arboretum in Lake County boasts one of the largest collections of rhododendron and azalea shrubs in North America.

James A. Garfield purchased this house in Mentor, named Lawnfield, in 1876 to accommodate his large family. He was elected president in 1880.

RIGHT PAGE: *Near North Kingsville, in Ashtabula County, shale bluffs tower more than ninety feet over the Lake Erie shoreline.*

President Garfield's term was the second-shortest in U.S. history: he served just over six months before he was assassinated.

Garfield campaigned vigorously from his home in Mentor and, after winning the election, used his home as an office to set up his new administration.

BEACHES ALONG THE LAKE ERIE SHORELINE

In the 1970s, a local rock group called the Euclid Beach Band wrote a Beach Boys–styled song that became a smash hit in the region. "There's No Surf in Cleveland" was a pop-twanged lament decrying the lack of beach culture in northeast Ohio. But these days, lighter surfboards and bodyboards as well as windsurfing boards bring the occasional enthusiast out for a try at Lake Erie's sometimes-challenging waves. Otherwise, sun worshipers make their way to the shoreline to enjoy the sights, sounds, and scents of the beach.

The Mentor Headlands at Headlands Beach State Park provides the largest beached area in the state for swimmers, with more than a mile of sandy shoreline. The sharp-eyed will also notice some plant species growing here that would otherwise only be found on the East Coast. Visitors to nearby Geneva-on-the-Lake State Park and Resort can take advantage of the park's diminutive swimming beach. And, just west of Mentor, the Cleveland Lakefront State Park operates two decidedly more urban beach locales, Edgewater Park and Euclid Beach Park. Both offer sandy beaches and lifeguards on duty during the summer.

East Harbor State Park, in the western portion of the state near Lakeside and Marblehead, operates a 1,500-foot sand beach, and visitors to Maumee Bay State Park in Toledo can sink their toes into the sandy stuff at the park's lakefront beach or at an inland lake within walking distance of the beach.

Reporters literally camped out on his lawn, waiting for his next campaign speech from the porch. A tour of the home and its property gives insight into the Garfield family and the times during which they lived. Complete with a guesthouse, chicken coop, and windmill, the home features the first presidential library, developed by Mrs. Garfield after her husband's death, inaugurating a tradition for presidents that persists to this day.

Ohioans, at least in this section of the state, talk politics and religion with some authority. Just south of the Garfield site is the Kirtland Temple, a building that almost overpowers the sleepy town of Kirtland. Built as the first temple of the Church of Latter-day Saints, this massive structure is a product of local stone quarries and lumberyards, as well as the labor of many. Construction began in 1833 and was finished in 1836. A mixture of Greek, Georgian, Gothic, and Federal architecture, the Kirtland Temple was

WINE TRAILS

Though there are wineries throughout the state, it's the Lake Erie region that hosts the most vintners. The rich soil and longer growing season afforded by the lake compelled many settlers in the New World to plant rows of grapes with the hope of a successful fall harvest.

These days, Ohio wines—particularly whites and champagnes—win accolades and awards internationally, and the winery boom is a great tourist attraction. Each August, Lake Farmpark hosts Vintage Ohio, a weekend-long tasting event featuring local and regional wine (and food). But most of the region's wineries welcome visitors at all times of the year and enjoy taking enthusiasts on property tours and tasting expeditions.

More than a dozen wineries in Lake County, Ohio, produce award-winning wines from Concord, Catawba, and other grape varieties.

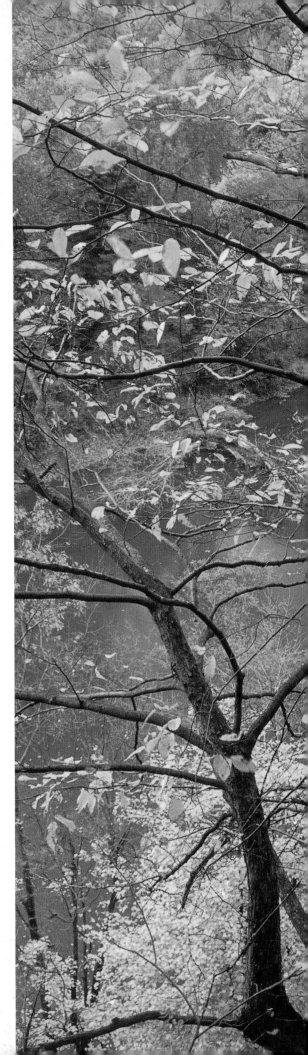

Lake County's Indian Point, the site of a former Whittlesey Culture Indian settlement, provides a spectacular view of the Grand River.

the largest building in the region at the time it was built. Inside, four sets of pulpits sit at the front and back ends of the main and second floors, and the pews were constructed to shift so that the congregation could comfortably view the front or back pulpits. Visitors should reserve some time to spend here admiring the architecture and craftsmanship.

A few miles south of the temple, Holden Arboretum celebrates nature's craftsmanship. Paths suitable for short strolls or sturdy hikes wind through a plethora of flora and fauna, and almost any time of the year is ideal for a visit. In late April to mid-May, more than 160 varieties of crabapple trees blossom, creating an intoxicating scent in the air and an engaging treat for the eyes—sensory overload at its best. And since Kirtland lies in the middle of the region's storied "snow belt," fans of the white stuff will enjoy a wintertime visit to the arboretum as well.

Kirtland has much to offer fans of the great outdoors. Penitentiary Glen and Chapin Forest lie just across the road from the arboretum, and a few miles south, visitors can explore the green acres of Lake Farmpark, a vibrant place where education and recreation collide. Visitors can learn about farming, agriculture, and animals—and pick up some science, too—with plenty of hands-on activities that include milking cows, making cheese, and tapping maple trees for the sap.

Head north and then east on Ohio Route 2, known also as Lakeland Parkway, to the lakeside town of Fairport Harbor. A sandy beach and the nation's first Great Lakes lighthouse museum make a visit here worthwhile. The box-shaped lighthouse served the shipping industry along Lake Erie for one hundred years. Visitors are welcome to climb the winding staircase for a view of the harbor, which in summer is busy with pleasure-boat traffic. The lighthouse museum houses the accoutrements of sea-faring adventurers who passed through the harbor over the years: relics from sailing ships, historical nautical equipment, and memorabilia from the town's nautical past.

Though Fairport Harbor has a nice beach, locals covet the mile-long stretch of beach and dunes at the nearby Headlands Beach State Park. The largest beach in Ohio, this attraction is a hot spot for the sun-starved in summer, but it's also a place of exploration for those interested in wildlife. Headlands Dunes State Nature Preserve, adjacent to the park, provides a rare glimpse of dune grasses and wildlife along the lake. Similarly, the Mentor Lagoons Nature Preserve protects some of the last marshland along the Lake Erie coastline.

Lake Erie's impact on the weather along the coastline wasn't lost on early settlers who wanted a glass of wine with their dinner. They realized that this climate was perfect for growing grapes, and the town of Madison (east of Fairport Harbor off U.S. Route 20) is home to the state's largest estate winery, Chalet Debonné Vineyards. Summertime visitors arrive for tours, tastings, and meals on the winery's lovely outdoor front porch, but wintertime enthusiasts can take part in the vineyard's ice wine harvest—they'd love a helping hand. Madison is a quaint little town, too. Stop at a historic bank-turned-teahouse for a sobering cup of tea after a visit to the winery.

Eastward along U.S. 20, Geneva-on-the-Lake is a town steeped in history and lively with new development. Geneva-on-the-Lake was founded in the late 1860s as Ohio's first summer resort. Legend has it that John D. Rockefeller, Henry Ford, and Harvey Firestone ventured here in the summer to spend some recreational time together. The town maintains a late-nineteenth-century charm to this day, welcoming visitors to its shores for festivals and events throughout the high season.

Geneva State Park and Resort brings a dose of the new to town, having recently built an up-to-date lodge and conference center on an open green space along the lakeshore. Modern and inviting, the affordable facility is just right for vacationing families, and the lodge's wine-tasting room celebrates regional vintages throughout the year.

As you travel a bit farther east on U.S. 20, suburban neighborhoods give way to farmland kept rich and moist by the many creeks and rivers that flow toward Lake Erie, which explains the sixteen covered bridges in this picturesque corner of the state. Each October, the town of Ashtabula celebrates its bridges with a festival, but any time of the year is appropriate for driving along the backroads of Ashtabula County to enjoy a look at these historical structures. Before going, visit www.coveredbridgefestival.org to request a driving tour map; it provides detailed information about how to get to each bridge and what you'll find when you get there.

Be sure to also visit Ashtabula's Marine Museum, an ongoing project to restore and preserve the Ashtabula Lighthouse and the maritime history of the area. Similarly, the city of Ashtabula is working hard to preserve and maintain its bascule—meaning "counterbalanced"—lift bridge, one of only five such lift bridges in the United States.

This route winds up in the northeastern corner of the state in the quiet town of Conneaut. Visit the town's downtown shops and eateries, or simply stroll by the lake.

CLEVELAND'S EMERALD NECKLACE
AN HEIRLOOM JEWEL ADORNING THE CITY

Cleveland's emerald necklace rings the city with an abundance of trails, nature centers, a zoo, paved bike paths, and lush greenery. The park system is considered to contain Cleveland's most treasured resources. Eighty miles of roads lead through twenty thousand acres of parks, beginning in the western suburb of Rocky River and extending south to Hinckley, then north again to Chagrin on the east side of town.

Begin a tour of the park system with breakfast at Sweetwater Landing, a nautical-themed restaurant open May through September that provides a view of the Rocky River and the Lake Erie water traffic that passes by in the summertime. Head south along Valley Parkway, noting the high shale cliffs that line either side of what locals call "the Valley." Turn up to Stinchcomb-Groth Memorial Scenic Overlook for a spectacular view of the reservation, which represents the first land purchase of the park system.

ROUTE 6

Start on Valley Parkway at the Detroit Road entrance near the Lakewood–Rocky River border. Take Valley Parkway south through Rocky River Reservation into Mill Stream Run Reservation. (An out-and-back side trip is available into Big Creek Reservation through Big Creek Parkway.) Continue on Valley Parkway to Brecksville Reservation. (Take State Road South for another out-and-back trip to Hinckley Reservation.) Exiting Brecksville Reservation, head north on Riverview Road, east on Alexander Road, and north on Dunham until you reach Gorge Parkway, which leads you through Bedford Reservation. From here, follow Hawthorn Parkway through South Chagrin Reservation to Sulphur Springs Drive. Chagrin River Road leads you to North Chagrin Reservation.

The Great Falls of Tinker's Creek, near Bedford Reservation south of Cleveland, is one of the largest waterfalls in the Buckeye State.

Birch tree roots cling to a sandstone outcrop in South Chagrin Reservation, near Chagrin Falls in Cuyahoga County.

Virginia bluebells carpet the woodlands in early spring at Rocky River Reservation in the western Cleveland suburbs.

The Brecksville Inn sheltered travelers during the western expansion but lost its fight for survival to suburban sprawl in 1999, when it was torn down to make way for commerce at the busy intersection of Ohio Routes 82 and 21 in Brecksville.

Oliver Hazard Perry's victory over the British on Lake Erie in the War of 1812 is memorialized in this statue at Cleveland Park.

Valley Parkway meanders south through the western suburbs of Cleveland, passing baseball diamonds, a horseback-riding facility, public golf courses, and the Rocky River Nature Center. Stop in the nature center for a quick hike on the boardwalk that lines the marshland, or take a challenging climb up the "mountain" for a great view of the winding river below.

From Valley Parkway, cut back to Big Creek Parkway in the Big Creek Reservation section of the park that winds through the city's southwestern suburbs. Lake Isaac is the big attraction here—particularly its waterfowl that forage for food and the wildlife sanctuary on its shores that provides a home for foxes, mink, and deer.

Double back to the Mill Stream Run Reservation, which encompasses the more powerful eastern branch of the Rocky River—a perfect spot for the mill-powered industries of the eighteenth and nineteenth centuries. Nearby quarries provided millstones, and the area flourished. But these days, power tobogganing attracts families, who take over the frozen toboggan chutes at the park's chalet during the cold months. Autumn brings hayrides around the chalet area.

To get to the southernmost area of the Cleveland Metroparks, it's necessary to leave the park system. Head south on Edgerton Road, turn right onto Ridge Road, and then go left on Weymouth Road into Hinckley Reservation. Each year, for at least the past two hundred years, buzzards arrive here on March 15 to nest in the park's high ledges and to hunt in its nearby fields. The town celebrates by greeting the buzzards with a festival. Throughout the rest of the year, however, it's Hinckley Lake that brings humans to the lake. Boaters can launch here, and visitors can rent canoes and kayaks for a paddle-powered tour of this picturesque lake. Hikers can explore the ledges and hunt for inscriptions and carvings left by eccentric locals.

To head to the Brecksville Reservation from Hinckley Lake, get back on Ohio Route 606 north, and turn right onto Ohio Route 303, heading east. This diverse section of the Metroparks features difficult hiking trails that lead from a floodplain dense with cottonwoods to ridge tops lined with oak-hickory forests. Seven distinctive gorges challenge those willing to take the trails. Visitors in vehicles can stop along the drive to take in the dramatic views.

The Metroparks then head north again, through Cleveland's eastern suburbs, into Bedford Reservation. Apparently, the two-hundred-foot gorge—a National Natural Landmark—and its rough terrain were too much for loggers who cut through the area, and this portion of the park is dense with trees. Visitors in the fall are welcomed by a splash of colors, scents, and the sound of crinkling leaves underfoot. Take a moment to stop at Tinkers Creek Gorge Scenic Overlook, which offers a fantastic view during any season.

In 1885, sculptor Henry Church carved Squaw Rock, which serves as a showpiece in the Chagrin Reservation section of the park. The sculpture is found at the southern end of the reservation and tells the story of hardship suffered by American Indians at the hands of European settlers.

Follow the Metroparks signs to the North Chagrin Reservation, a portion of the park that slices through Cleveland's tony eastern suburbs.

Beech foliage frames a birch tree's trunk at Tinker's Creek Overlook in Bedford Reservation.

This charming waterfall flows near Sulphur Springs Picnic Area in South Chagrin Reservation.

Henry Church sculpted this fanciful bas-relief of an American Indian woman and a snake in 1885 on a large block of Berea sandstone near the Chagrin River in South Chagrin Reservation.

Squires Castle is a popular curiosity; it was originally built as a gatehouse to a mansion that never materialized. But most people enjoy the marshlands that provide a home to waterfowl and dragonflies.

CUYAHOGA VALLEY NATIONAL PARK
RESTORING NATURE TO AN INDUSTRIAL LANDSCAPE

ROUTE 7

Begin at the Canal Visitor Center on Canal Road in Valley View. Follow Canal Road to Riverview Road throughout the park—maps and detailed directions to points of interest can be found at the Canal Visitor Center. Exiting the park in Akron, continue heading south on Riverview Road to Smith Road to visit Naturealm.

If the Cleveland Metroparks system is the town's heirloom emerald necklace, then the Cuyahoga Valley National Park is the city's new diamond bracelet. Dangling off the wrist of the southern tip of Cleveland, this wonderful national park extends all the way down to Akron, representing a shiny new bangle for the region to show off. Fought and lobbied for by grassroots organizations and politicians who sought to clean up a series of brownfields, the old canal system, and some unsightly industrial wastelands, the park grew from a few disparate cleanup campaigns into a canal restoration project, then a national recreation area, and finally a national park. It now encompasses a bike path that takes cyclists from Cleveland to Akron via the Canal Towpath Trail along a series of trails that includes Ohio's statewide Buckeye Trail; a hiking trail that leads hikers along pathways that connect to the Metroparks system and the Ohio Buckeye Trail; and a railway that takes visitors from depot to depot aboard historic trains. The trails provide a vital source of much-needed capital for historical sites, small towns, restaurants, and inns along the way.

Begin your journey through the Cuyahoga Valley National Park at the Canal Visitor Center, which is located in a home that used to service canal boat passengers and crew waiting to pass through the system of forty-four locks that lifted to an elevation of 395 feet the canal boats traveling between Cleveland and Akron. The visitor center tells the story of the park through exhibits and a slide show and it offers a great starting point where visitors can get maps, information, and souvenirs.

The main road through the park is the Canal Way Ohio National Scenic Byway. Along with the main trails and train tracks, this road follows the path of the Cuyahoga River and the Ohio and Erie Canal.

Almost all the historic sites along the waterway were built with the hope of opportunity for commerce along the river and, later, the canal, and the sites along the byway tell the story of commerce in the area from the 1800s on. Just south of the visitor center you'll find Tinker's Creek Aqueduct, built in the early 1900s and one of four aqueducts in the Cuyahoga Valley. A bit farther south, Alexander's Mill demonstrates how progress was made along the river. Originally a traditional river-powered mill where flour was ground, the mill was later installed with a turbine to make more efficient use of waterpower, and then was switched from a flour mill to a feed mill. Operations continued at the mill into the 1970s.

A few minutes south of the mill, the Frazee House predates the canal, having been constructed in 1826 as a residence in the Western Reserve style. It now serves as an excellent archeological research tool and a visitor center.

Originally built as a residence and later used as a tavern for canal travelers, the Frazee House now functions as a tourist attraction and an archeological site that provides valuable clues into life along the canals.

INNER-CITY WILDERNESS

Taking a walk through the Cleveland Metroparks Zoo is really more like enjoying a hike through the wilderness—in the middle of the industrial neighborhood of Cleveland. Much like the rest of the Metroparks system, the zoo is nicely integrated with the landscape, providing all the traditional sights and sounds of a zoo while maintaining the look and feel of a park. A walk through the zoo is a workout as you meander from monkey house to big-cat exhibits to bear houses via a picturesque trail. Interactive and fun, the 165-acre zoo is home to more than three thousand animals and features lively programming throughout the year. Also on the zoo property is the Rainforest, an indoor exhibit (perfect for winter escapes), which provides visitors with a tropical experience. Animals live in their natural habitats, which include hundreds of varieties of tropical plants, trees, and shrubs, all in a moist, tropical environment.

The village of Peninsula lies about halfway between the northern terminus of the Cuyahoga Valley Scenic Railroad at Rockside Road, south of Cleveland and the southern terminus at Quaker Square in Akron.

Cows graze in a pasture at Hale Farm and Village, a reconstructed Civil War–era pioneer settlement in Cuyahoga Valley National Park.

This Cuyahoga Valley wetland was an old car dump before it was cleaned up by the National Park Service in the 1970s. Beavers moved in and completed the wetland restoration, and today the area is a popular destination for birds and bird-watchers.

South of the Frazee House, Cuyahoga Valley National Park connects with the Cleveland Metroparks' Brecksville Reservation.

Cuyahoga Valley National Park features a number of waterfalls, three of which are clustered in the middle of the park. Blue Hen Falls is accessible by a hiking trail, as is Buttermilk Falls, which is nearby but easy to miss. But if you have time to see only one waterfall in the park, make sure to visit Brandywine Falls to view its sixty-foot drop. Accessed by a picturesque walking path, Brandywine Falls offers a glimpse at the Inn at Brandywine Falls, a lovely old farmhouse bed and breakfast that is also home to a few horses who gallop back and forth inside white fencing. Book well in advance if you want to secure a room at this popular overnight spot, or consider a stay for less money at the Hostelling International Stanford House, a lovely 1830s farmhouse. With rates as low as $15 a night, the Stanford House is a bargain—and it's a nice midway point between Cleveland and Akron. Two ski resorts—Boston Mills and Brandywine—are close by, making the Stanford House an excellent destination for winter sports enthusiasts.

One of the park's most interactive features is Hale Farm and Village. Depicting life in Wheatville, Ohio, during the time of the Civil War, the farm features on-site blacksmiths, glassblowers, and regular folk who tell their stories to visitors while they perform chores, cook johnnycake, and fret about life on the frontier. A time-honored tradition for years, Hale Farm is closed during the winter months, but its accurate period architecture makes it worth a drive through even when it's snowing.

As is so often the case in the Rust Belt, the industrialists who brought commerce here—and in a roundabout way who polluted the area—were also the benefactors who donated land for civic parks and who endowed trusts to preserve them. At the northern tip of the Ohio and Erie Canal Corridor, John D. Rockefeller bestowed parklands that became the basis of Cleveland's cultural center. At the southern tip of the canal corridor, F. A. Seiberling, founder of the Goodyear Tire and Rubber Company, left his mark on the landscape with Naturealm, a park that features a unique underground visitor center and a sixteen-acre arboretum. Walkways and paths are accessible to all. The Cleveland Metroparks end a bit south of Naturealm, but the scenic byway extends into Tuscarawas County, where the canal meets the Tuscarawas River, allowing its traffic (in the old days) to continue its journey toward the Ohio River.

RUST BELT TOUR
VESTIGES OF THE STEEL INDUSTRY

Between Warren and Bellaire in Ohio's northeastern industrial region, the landscape is dotted with factories and evidence of better days, but there is also plenty of beauty. Here the rolling hills of the Appalachian Plateau provide a sense of diversity and the roads meander through valleys and rich

ROUTE 8

Begin at the Trumbull County Courthouse in downtown Warren and take State Route 82 east to State Route 11 south to Youngstown, then continue south on Route 11 and head west on State Route 344 to Leetonia. Continue on Route 11 south to State Route 154 west to visit Lisbon, and then follow U.S. Route 30 west to Hanoverton. Backtrack on Route 30 and head east to East Liverpool. Drive south on State Route 7 through Steubenville, Mingo Junction, and Martins Ferry to Bellaire. Just north of Tiltonsville, State Route 150 provides a side trip to Mount Pleasant.

The Trumbull County Courthouse casts an imposing shadow over the downtown Warren skyline. The building was dedicated in 1897, and the courthouse's first "statue of justice" was dedicated on the day of Ohioan William McKinley's inauguration.

farmland. Many immigrants from Germany and the Alsace region staked a claim here, happy to find a climate and countryside so similar to their own. Their industrious nature introduced a healthy work ethic into the area, and from the potteries of East Liverpool to the coke ovens of Leetonia to the storied steel mills of Youngstown, this region is known for its productivity as well as its beauty.

Pride in place is evident at the Trumbull County Courthouse in Warren. The monstrous Richardsonian-Romanesque building constructed in 1895 looks more like a European castle than an American courthouse. Inside its stone walls, Clarence Darrow argued cases and Susan B. Anthony kept offices. When steel workers were locked out of the WCI Steel Plan in Warren in 1995, more than seven thousand workers showed up on the courthouse lawn in protest.

In 1997 the building was restored, and a tour of its interior reveals ornate carved-wood walls, lovingly restored ironwork, and amazing lighting fixtures. The beautiful building is the centerpiece of a district teeming with more than two hundred historically significant structures.

A bird's-eye view of Steubenville is seen from a hillside across the Ohio River in West Virginia. Steubenville was originally called Fort Steuben, named for Baron von Steuben, a Prussian soldier who helped train General George Washington's Continental Army.

The towers of Wheeling Pittsburgh Steel Corporation loom over the town of Mingo Junction in Jefferson County in the heart of Ohio's Rust Belt. Scenes from the movie The Deer Hunter *were filmed here.*

Steubenville is known as the City of Murals. More than thirty historical murals have been painted on the walls of city buildings during the past two decades.

Ohio Route 422 leads directly from Warren into Youngstown's Mill Creek Metroparks. Encompassing 2,600 acres of land alongside Mill Creek, this park has everything from T-ball diamonds to two eighteen-hole Donald Ross championship golf courses. Visitors to the park shouldn't miss a stroll through Fellows Riverside Gardens. Eleven acres of annuals and perennials have thrived here since the garden was dedicated in 1963; when the roses are in bloom, the air carries their scent. A wildlife preserve and wetlands area round out this park, which can run from rustic to perfectly manicured, depending on which of the twenty miles of park road you're driving on.

Equally significant in Youngstown is the Butler Institute of American Art. The museum houses the works of artists ranging from Winslow Homer to Georgia O'Keefe. It was the first museum in the United States built specifically to house works by our nation's artists. In addition to an overwhelming collection of portraits, landscapes, and other traditional American art, the museum features a children's gallery and a gallery dedicated to sports art—pleasing everyone in the car.

Once you've seen the charcoal drawings at the Butler Institute, check out the process of charcoal burning at the Cherry Valley Coke Ovens Arboretum in Leetonia. These beehive-shaped ovens were constructed to burn the impurities out of coal, creating coke, the fuel needed to burn fires hot enough to manufacture iron and steel. More than two hundred ovens were in operation here from the 1860s until the Great Depression. Now the ovens are on the National Register of Historic Places.

The drive south from Youngstown delivers two diverse viewpoints of the state. At times the area seems rural and bucolic, and then suddenly industrial sites and factories emerge, delivering an entirely different perspective on the region. With its rivers, railroads, canal systems, and the Lincoln Highway, this part of the country was a crossroads of goods, industry, and people almost from the moment settlers began crossing the mountains.

At Lisbon, swing west for a quick drive along the well-marked Lincoln Highway. Lisbon, the second-oldest town in Ohio, is filled with kitsch. Old diners with true roadside character can be found—some are open, some aren't—and the Old Stone House Tavern, just a block off the highway, is the second-oldest continuously occupied stone house in the state. Lisbon was a strong abolitionist town. It is also noted as the birthplace of the paper straw.

A few miles west of Lisbon along the Lincoln Highway you'll pass through the town of Hanoverton, which proudly touts its historic district on Plymouth Street. Containing twenty Federal-style homes listed on the National Register of Historic Places, this district has a distinctive feel of Georgetown right on the edge of Ohio. The Spread Eagle Tavern also maintains its spot in history, welcoming guests for an overnight stay or for a bite to eat in one of its seven dining rooms—and, good news to weary travelers, the Spread Eagle serves lunch and dinner every day of the week.

Double back on the Lincoln Highway to experience the rural setting of Beaver Creek State Park, named for the Sandy and Beaver Canal that carried traffic to the Ohio and Erie Canal. One of the canal's most significant locks features a double-curved stone staircase and is considered one of the most artistic canals in Ohio's canal system.

With the rich clay found in the floodplain of the mighty Ohio, this region became home to a significant pottery industry. The story of the region's grounding in clay is told at the Museum of Ceramics in East Liverpool. From the mid-1800s until the Depression, more than half of the nation's pottery was produced in East Liverpool. The museum collection, housed in the town's old post office, showcases both the process and the end products of the craft.

South of East Liverpool, the road follows the Ohio River and is marked as an Ohio River Scenic Byway. The little finger of West Virginia's western edge creeps up here between the Ohio and Pennsylvania border.

Known as the City of Murals, Steubenville sports floodwalls worthy of a long afternoon stroll. Twenty-five murals depict the history of the town in vibrant color. Larger than life and eerily realistic, mural scenes pop off of their backdrops to illustrate pioneer life along the river and show men working in the foundries. Of course, the town's favorite son, Dean Martin, has his own space on this wall of fame. This Rat Pack celeb was born and raised in Steubenville, and the town holds a festival in his honor every June. Those who can't make it to the festival can take a walking tour to some of Martin's favorite local haunts.

On South Third Street, Steubenville's pivotal role in history is again celebrated. It was here that Fort Steuben was erected to serve as a base of protection for the surveyors sent to map the Northwest Territory. Originally built in 1786, the fort was reconstructed in the late 1980s to celebrate the role Steubenville played as a conduit to the New Frontier.

Following the scenic byway along the river, travelers receive constant reminders of industry. For enthusiasts of old steel mills and film noir buffs, Mingo Junction is worth a stop. Miles of train track, the grit of outdated manufacturing plants, oversized piping connected to industrial buildings, and smokestacks stretching tall into the sky give the town a decidedly tough character.

It's quite a juxtaposition, then, to travel only twenty miles farther and arrive in the charming town of Mount Pleasant. Settled by Quakers, Mount Pleasant features early American architecture lovingly maintained in the town's historic district. The most distinctive structure in town is the Quaker Yearly Meeting House, constructed in 1814. The building could accommodate two thousand visitors and was considered an architectural marvel in its day. Many feel it still is, and the meetinghouse now serves as a state memorial, celebrating not only the town and its architecture but the Quakers who lived here, lobbied for abolition, and played a crucial role in the Underground Railroad.

The road gets busy again as the highway enters Martin's Ferry, but travel a few more miles south to the town of Bellaire, where the Interstate Toll Bridge looms 350 feet above the Ohio River. Seven million pounds of steel were fused together to connect Bellaire, Ohio, to Benwood, West Virginia. If it looks familiar, rent *The Silence of the Lambs* again—the bridge enjoyed its fifteen minutes of fame in a scene in this now-classic thriller.

Gaston's Mill was built by Samuel Conkle in 1837 along the Sandy and Beaver Canal, north of East Liverpool in Columbiana County. The mill is preserved with other canal-era structures, including a restored canal lock, in Beaver Creek State Park.

An extensive collection of roses enhance the views at Fellows Riverside Gardens, part of Mill Creek Park in the western suburbs of Youngstown.

Founded by Quakers in 1800, Mount Pleasant in Jefferson County was the site of Ohio's first abolitionist convention, held in 1837. President Abraham Lincoln's secretary of war, Edwin Stanton, was born here in December 1814.

ROUTE 9

Begin at the Geauga County Courthouse in Chardon and take State Route 44 south to U.S. Route 322 west to State Route 306 south to Chagrin Falls. Then follow State Route 87 east to Punderson State Park, Burton, Middlefield, and Mesopotamia.

The northeast Ohio metropolitan media market is ranked the seventeenth-largest in the nation, with a population of almost three million people. Cleveland and Akron bustle with urban life and the suburbs are crowded with homes and apartments. Even the "bigger" towns like Chagrin Falls fight hard against urban sprawl, their zoning boards hosting hot debates over whether or not to allow big-box retailers inside the city limits. Yet less than thirty minutes from the heart of either city's downtown district, farmhouses sit quietly in fields, with candles flickering in the windows instead of electric lights, and the mode of transportation is horse-drawn buggies instead of SUVs.

This northeast section of Ohio is known as the "snow belt"; when the conditions are right, holidays in towns like Chardon and Chagrin are infused with an extra dose of puffy white charm. Chardon puts on the dog in early April, when it hosts the Geauga County Maple Festival, honoring the syrup industry that has been so good to the town since its earliest days, and providing an attractive diversion to snow-belters who have been holed

The class of 1914 assembles on the lawn at Hiram College. The college originally opened as the Western Reserve Eclectic Institute in 1850.

Chardon's Bass Lake Hotel served as a playground hangout for Clevelanders on vacation in this small town in the late 1800s.

Eastlawn Cemetery at Mantua Center in Portage County lies in the heart of northeast Ohio's Western Reserve. In the background are the civic center, a Christian church, and an 1840s town house.

The Windsor Mills Covered Bridge was built over rugged Phelps Creek in 1867 west of Windsor in Ashtabula County. Ashtabula County is the largest county in Ohio and has sixteen covered bridges—more than any other county in the Buckeye State.

up in their homes all winter long. When in Chardon, don't miss the Geauga County Courthouse, built to complement the existing architecture in the town during the post–Civil War period. Stones and bricks make up the High Victorian–Italianate styling that now serves as the centerpiece of the town's Courthouse Historic Square District.

If "be charming" isn't listed in Chagrin Falls' town charter, it ought to be. More than eighty shops line the downtown streets, which have symbolized "cute" for generations. As if the backdrop of the Chagrin River's waterfalls weren't enough to entice visitors to come, the streets of Chagrin Falls are currently receiving a facelift, and visitors will soon be treated to decorative streetlamps and brick-paved walkways. There's always a good view of the falls from street level, but during the non-icy months, take the stairs down to the bottom of the falls to really enjoy the river. When you're done, hike back up the stairs and visit the town's immortal Popcorn Shop, a sweets and candy stop, for a scoop of ice cream.

Southwest of Chardon, Newbury Township has its roots in early American history; it's named for a land surveyor who liked the area so much that he became the town's first settler. It was also one of the first hot spots for the suffragist movement. In the late 1920s, construction began on Punderson Manor, an English Tudor–style home along Punderson Lake that was later purchased by the Ohio Parks and Recreation Department and turned into a lodge. These days, Punderson State Park thrives around the lake, and the lodge maintains the intellectual traditions started by the New England settlers who arrived on the shores of the lake two hundred years ago. The studious-looking Tudor mansion is a favorite spot for artists' and writers' conferences.

A maple syrup center, the town of Burton loves its sweets; even the gas stations have the freshest maple-glazed products you'll find for miles around. When touring the town, which sits just east of Punderson, be sure to walk the town square. Century Village has collected one hundred years of area history right in the middle of town. A cabin from the late 1700s, a schoolhouse from the late 1800s, and a host of curiosities from the years in-between all lie within walking distance of each other, bringing the history of the area to life in an easy-to-navigate area. Just next door to Century Village, the newly constructed Red Maple Inn blends in nicely with the village and gives visitors two more reasons to stay in Burton for an evening: wonderful meals cooked by the inn's Mennonite kitchen staff and fantastic views of the Cuyahoga Valley.

Burton Wetlands State Nature Preserve features a series of ponds and wetlands left largely undisturbed since the glaciers created the landscape thousands of years ago. Like nearby Punderson Lake, Lake Kelso was carved into the landscape by a melting glacier. Conditions were right for the twenty-two-acre lake to take on a bog environment ideal for the growth of beautiful orchids and not-so-enticing poison sumac. Stick to the marked trails here or you might be sorry.

The town of Middlefield, which hosts a strong Amish population, built its reputation on Swiss cheese. The art of cheese making is celebrated in factory tours, while local shops sell handmade crafts. Swine Creek Reservation celebrates the county's favorite pastime at the sugarhouse, where sap is typically boiling on weekends during March, and the atmosphere is made more festive with horse-drawn wagon rides, blazing fires indoors and out, and a skating rink in the winter months.

The town of Mesopotamia, due east of Middlefield, is home to one of the state's oldest general stores still in operation. The End of the Commons General Store sells handicrafts, candies, and bulk foods within a historical setting. A tourist hot spot, Mesopotamia makes a good base from which to explore Amish Country attractions. Visit the general store to get information about hard-to-find shops or to find out about local families who host dinners in their homes. The town is also home to a peculiar octagonal house, on Noble Road just south of town.

Throughout the planting and harvesting seasons, the countryside comes alive with cows grazing on fresh grass, fertile fields, and the scents of the season. Since its inception in the 1850s, Hiram College has provided a liberal education to students on its decidedly New Englandy campus. Students often leave campus to visit Nelson Kennedy Ledges State Park, just east of the school, where dramatic rock formations and sandstone cliffs once towered over an important trading post for the American Indian population and later served as a landmark for the earliest settlers. The nearby town of Garrettsville became the first mill town in the region, positioning the town as a center of commerce for years to come.

End this backroads journey with a loop through the Windsor Mills Covered Bridge. The oldest remaining covered bridge in the country, this 120-foot-long bridge was constructed in 1867 and refurbished in 2004.

PART III

CENTRAL OHIO
OHIO'S HEARTLAND

FACING PAGE:
The covered bridge that spans the Mohican River at Clearfork Gorge in Mohican State Park has a steel truss and is a modern testament to the old wooden covered bridges that once were prolific in the area.

ABOVE:
Wheat sheaves line fields north of Berlin in Holmes County, the heart of the world's largest Amish population, in north-central Ohio.

Central Ohio is, in many ways, America's crossroads. The National Road cuts right through the state's center and was the first and most widely used route from the East to the West. Early explorers, land agents, and ambitious settlers crossed through the state as they made their way to the new land, some settling here as others moved on.

This was the stomping ground for Johnny Appleseed, an ambitious entrepreneur who built apple tree nurseries and planted apple orchards, anticipating the needs of the population on the move. Other heroic figures, from American Indian legends to Revolutionary and Civil War heroes to modern-day space explorers, have called central Ohio home.

The earliest people in the region left their mark on the land in the form of mounds that remain to this day, drawing visitors who admire the ingenuity of the formations or who seek spirituality from the sites. American Indian culture thrived on the bountiful plains of central Ohio, and place names, historic sites, and legends prevail throughout the region. One romantic, Zane Grey, loved the tales of cowboys and Indians so much he wrote the stories down, giving birth to the modern American Western novel.

But it was the industrious early settlers who gave this region a flair for no-nonsense hard work that persists to this day. Exploring villages settled by the Amish, Mennonites, Zoar Separatists, and even Swedenborgs—who claimed Johnny Appleseed as their best ombudsman in the New World—gives visitors a sense of the faith, determination, and strength of the people who established Ohio.

Today, the central portion of the state offers visitors diverse options. Rolling hills in the northern portion of central Ohio teem with rivers, parklands, and historic sites. In the center of the state, the land flattens and the commerce that buzzes around Columbus quickly gives way to a rural setting outside the city limits. Exploring the National Road is like driving through a diorama of American history, but don't neglect to veer south toward the more mystic regions of central Ohio to discover its charms too.

HOLMES AND TUSCARAWAS COUNTIES' RURAL TOUR
RURAL OHIO AT ITS BEST

ROUTE 10

Begin in Zoar and take State Route 212 south to State Route 800 south to State Route 416 south to New Philadelphia. Follow 4th Street north toward Dover, and pick up State Route 39 west to Sugar Creek and Berlin.

In Holmes and Tuscarawas counties, the most unlikely groups of cultures merged, creating a wealth of unique experiences within the same landscape. Within the space of these two counties, it's possible to learn about American Indian history, German culture, the Schoenbrunn movement, Switzerland's impact on the area, and Amish and Mennonite cultures. It's hard to find a road in this region that hasn't been declared a scenic byway by one agency or another. Straying from the main roads and getting lost here is half the fun of exploring the region. The main roads are lined with antique shops, Amish-themed stores, and roadside stands, but the roads less taken allow a

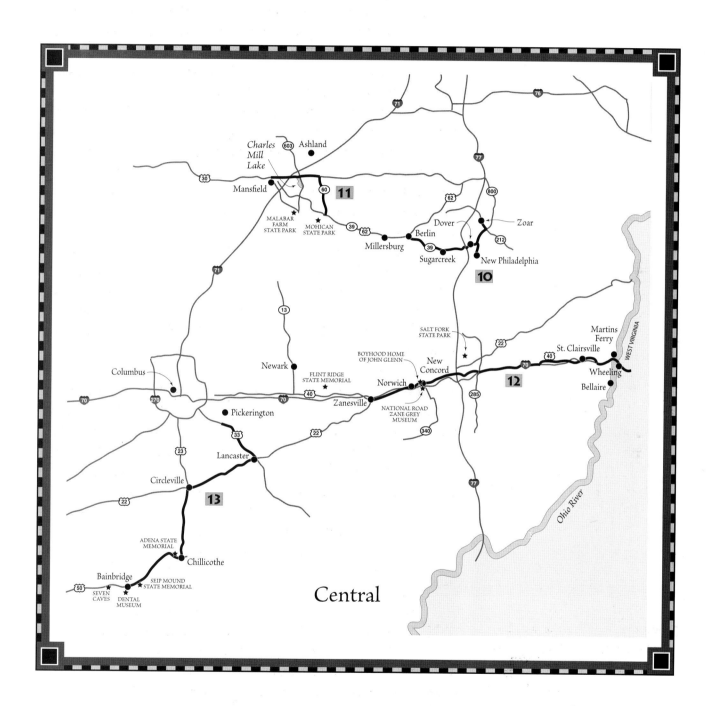

Central

Magnolia Flouring Mill was constructed by Richard Elson in 1834 along the Sandy and Beaver Canal in Magnolia, Stark County. Today the mill is managed by his great-grandson Mack Elson.

Magnolias bloom in early spring at the United Church of Christ, which occupies the 1856 meetinghouse at Zoar Village in Tuscarawas County.

Rose mallows bloom in midsummer in the main gardens at Zoar Village. The community was founded in 1817 by Joseph Baumeler and other separatists fleeing religious persecution in their native Germany.

Greetings from Zoar Ohio. Zoar Hotel.

The historic town of Zoar still operates a traditional hotel and restaurant with guest rooms on the second floor.

glimpse of truly rural life and, every so often, yield a surprise produce stand or a local eatery waiting to be explored.

Pick up some freshly ground cornmeal at the Magnolia Flouring Mill, a three-and-a-half story bright-red mill run by generations of the Elson family. The mill has flourished since the 1830s by following that time-honored real-estate principal, "location, location, location." Situated on the Sandy and Beaver Canal, the mill once enjoyed access to a railroad line, which helped it survive while other mills died out.

Two types of settlers arrived in this region of Ohio: families like the Elsons who came here to forge a better living, and settlers who sought to break away from the problems presented when politics and religion were mixed in their countries of origin. Towns along this route give testimony to the Europeans who immigrated here in order to worship as they pleased.

Many of these towns are beginning to reconnect with the homelands of their settlers. After traveling to the Alsace, for example, locals installed new window boxes, bright with geraniums, at the Zoar Tavern in Zoar Village. The landscape in this region bears an uncanny resemblance in appearance, climate, and style to its "mother" region of the Alsace. It's no wonder that the Society of Separatists of Zoar chose this region for their communal village in the early 1800s. Unlike many of the restored villages in Ohio, Zoar has managed to integrate its living history museum with the idea of living historically. Drive into town and you might find it hard to distinguish which buildings are part of the museum tour and which are occupied by locals. Ten historic buildings reflecting the German-influenced architecture of the settlers are situated right in the middle of town. Maintained lovingly by the current community, gardens flourish in the "official" tour area, but travelers should stroll through town and see the historical homes, visit some of the area businesses, and grab a bite to eat at the Zoar Tavern.

Only a few miles from Zoar Village, more than three hundred Moravians settled Schoenbrunn Village in 1772, in what today is known as New Philadelphia. The original settlers acted as missionaries to the region's Delaware population and thrived until their refusal to take sides in the Revolutionary War led to their massacre in 1777. The Moravian village and way of life is reconstructed for visitors, showcasing buildings typical of the era and interpreting the lifestyle and work of the original settlers at a visitor center. An outdoor drama called *Trumpet in the Land* brings the story of Schoenbrunn to life, with the help of actors, horses, and special effects.

Downtown New Philadelphia maintains a lovely main street and is home to the Tuscarawas County Courthouse. Those interested in modern history might want to stop in the town's Quaker Stadium, where legendary Ohio State football coach Woody Hayes held his first job. And at the Harry Clever Airport, John Glenn's first solo airplane flight is celebrated.

North of New Philadelphia, in Dover, the townspeople like the idea of preserving their history. Victorian homes along its prosperous streets survived hard times and are well kept—some are on the National Register of Historic Places. But the most beloved tradition in town is found at the Warther Carving Museum, where fourth-generation Warthers continue a tradition that began here in the 1920s when Ernest Warther whittled his way to the title "World's Master Carver." His precise, intricate works in ivory and wood include miniature locomotives, ornate canes designed for presidents, and a working replica of a steel mill. His work is showcased at the Smithsonian and also here in Dover. The Warther Carving Museum also manufactures knives that visitors can buy on the premises.

Eleven miles west of Dover, the village of Sugarcreek is known as "Ohio's Little Switzerland." Driving into town, you're bombarded by a particular brand of kitsch developed specifically for tourists in the 1950s and 1960s, but the heaping dose of charm is a welcome sight. Heavily populated by German Americans, Amish, and Mennonites, the town maintains a high level of old-country charm, evoking the Alps amidst Ohio's comparatively smaller hills through an annual festival, cheese factory tours, and plenty of shops where local and German-influenced crafts are sold.

Belgian horses, seen here grazing near Mount Hope in Holmes County, are favored by the Amish for their great strength and gentle disposition.

Amish craftsmen raise a large barn, using only hand tools, in less than a day near Mount Hope in Ohio's Amish Country.

West of Sugarcreek, the main roads leading to Walnut Creek, Berlin, and Millersburg deliver a patchwork of farm fields interrupted by small towns that thrive on the Amish tourist trade. The town of Walnut Creek bustles with activity throughout the year. It's a great stop for anyone looking for Amish furniture or antiques, fresh cheese, patio furniture, or garden implements. Overnight accommodations abound here, from charming family-run bed and breakfasts to the newly constructed Carlisle Inn, a modern hotel on a hill.

The nearby town of Berlin features a little less bustle but the same type of charm. Take a tour of the Amish and Mennonite Heritage Center for an accurate picture of how these cultures in the region live and work, or tour a working farm. But be sure to drive along the country roads that surround Berlin; the farmhouses, barns, and real-life scenes of Amish tilling the land and kids playing in the fields is well worth the time.

Daydreamers who drive through this part of the state might get swept up in the romanticism of country living, and Lehman's hardware store is there to feed the dream. Originally opened in the 1950s to provide appliances and hardware to the non-electricity-using Amish population, this store has developed a national reputation for providing goods to cottage dwellers, simple-life enthusiasts, and those seeking hard-to-find items for the home. A national catalog services a wide variety of customers, but a tour of the shop inspires ideas that could lead to a new fireplace—or a lifestyle change.

End your tour of Amish country at the Inn at Honey Run. This unusual inn, set in the woods just outside Millersburg, serves upscale meals in its main dining room. Overnight guests can stay in the inn's main building or book a honeycomb suite, a series of structures in the side of a hill, set away from the main building. The inn's property is crisscrossed with many marked and unmarked trails.

MANSFIELD AREA
OLD INDIAN TALES AND TRAILS

ROUTE 11

Begin this tour at Kingwood Center in Mansfield. Then follow U.S. Route 30 east to State Route 60 south and continue on to Loudonville.

It can be difficult to choose which time of year is best to visit Mansfield. Its wealth of gardens and parks make it an excellent springtime drive; its waterways, liveries, hotels, and state parks are tailor-made for summer visitors; and forests bulging with tall trees draw visitors here for autumn leaf-peeping. As the midway point between Cleveland and Columbus, this region is frequented by city dwellers, who find it a fine escape from urban life almost any time of year.

Throughout the year, the Kingwood Center in Mansfield invites guests to tour its mansion and public gardens. The opulent mansion, built in the 1920s, reflects the good taste and wealth of the King family, whose fortune was made on brass fittings. In the 1950s, they willed the estate grounds to be opened as a public garden space, and since that time, the center has served as a place for horticultural hobnobbing. Casual visitors stroll through the prolific gardens, while the more serious attend programs at the center.

During winter months, guests arrive to tour the mansion when it's dressed up for the holidays.

Holidaymakers enjoy downtown Mansfield's interesting cottage industry—carousels. Richland Carousel Park is home to the first hand-carved carousel built since the 1930s, while workers at nearby Carousel Magic demonstrate the craftsmanship needed to restore and build the magical storybook animals.

For a less magical experience, head north of downtown Mansfield to the Ohio State Reformatory. A vintage castle that formerly housed Ohio inmates, this building has been featured in three major movies, most notably *The Shawshank Redemption*. Abandoned in 1990, the imposing structure hosts tours—when it's not getting ready for a close-up, that is. Those who book early can claim a spot on an overnight tour of the reformatory that typically takes place around Halloween.

Hollywood again factors into the region just a few miles east of the reformatory, at Malabar Farm State Park. Malabar Farm, the home of screenwriter Louis Bromfield, played host to Bogie and Bacall's wedding in 1945. But the real attraction here is the farm and the farming techniques innovated by Bromfield. The farm's produce is sold at a roadside stand across the street, and the Malabar Inn—a restaurant—uses the field-fresh produce in its tasty dishes. Ambitious hikers can climb to the top of steep Mount Jeez, located near the restaurant, for a stunning view of the farm and fields below.

East of Mansfield, Charles Mill Lake Park is a beloved recreational facility. Boating, fishing, and camping are popular here. Johnny Appleseed walked through the forests and along the paths that hikers now enjoy in the park systems permeating the area. In Loudonville, Mohican State Park and Mohican State Memorial Forest give history and nature buffs a chance to retrace Appleseed's steps. Mohican is a lively park, filled during the warmer months with visitors who come for a day of canoeing or hiking, as well as overnight guests who make use of the park resort or a wealth of campgrounds and cottages on the property. Lyons Fall Trail follows the Clear Fork Gorge; hikers who make this journey enjoy the treat of seeing two waterfalls along the way. The park's Hemlock Trail leads to a covered bridge.

The Wolf Creek/Pine Run Grist Mill dates to the 1830s. Originally located on Wolf Creek, the mill was dismantled and moved to its present location on Pine Run in order to welcome visitors for tours. Though Ohio harbors a number of picturesque mills, this one, constructed of wood and featuring an overshot waterwheel, is run by volunteers, who answer questions while they operate the mill.

Fans of opulence should not miss Landoll Castle, a more recent addition to local lore. Built by a man who made his fortune illustrating and publishing fairy tale books, Loudonville's castle has the look and feel of an ancient fortress, with spires, towers, and dramatic architecture throughout. The property is operated as a very expensive hotel, but visitors are welcome to dine at the restaurant or browse through the shop without booking a room for the night.

*More than 35,000 tulips
and other spring bulbs
provide a spectacular
display for visitors to the
gardens at Kingwood
Center in Mansfield.*

A tiny spring peeper frog rests on a wild onion leaf among squirrel cornflowers blooming along a trail at Fowler Woods State Nature Preserve.

A male peacock struts among the floral displays at Kingwood Center, one of Ohio's most spectacular public gardens.

The Shawshank Redemption *is one of several movies that have been filmed in the grim buildings of the Ohio State Reformatory at Mansfield. Opened in 1896, the prison, which has the largest cell block ever built, was closed in 1990.*

After immersing in the area's natural wonders, consider bringing some home. Drive westward along Ohio Route 97 to the Wade and Gatton Nursery. The road winds through a forested area leading to Bellville. Display gardens at the nursery make this more than just a shopping trip—wander through the gardens for ideas or inspiration, and take a bit of the region home with you.

THE NATIONAL ROAD TOUR (EASTERN PORTION)
AMERICA'S FIRST ROAD OF COMMERCE

ROUTE 12

Most of this route follows U.S. Route 40, the National Road. Begin in Wheeling, West Virginia, and cross the Wheeling Suspension Bridge into Ohio, then follow the signs to U.S. 40 and drive west through Blaine. Continue heading west on the National Road through Saint Clairsville. On U.S. 40 near New Concord, the route is marked as the John Glenn Highway. Detour onto South Friendship Drive and continue on State Route 83 south to visit the Wilds, or stay on the National Road and head west to the National Road/Zane Grey Museum in Norwich. The Flint Ridge State Memorial is on Brownsville Road in Glenford, and the Dawes Arboretum is just off the National Road on Jacksontown Road.

Construction began on the National Road in 1811, with the idea of connecting American Indian routes and existing roads and stagecoach lines to cut a clear path from Maryland to St. Louis. Conestoga wagons wore down the path that later became U.S. Route 40 when automobiles arrived on the scene. As the oldest east-west route through the United States, this main artery to America's heartland contains layer upon layer of history.

Ohio's portion of the road begins on the Wheeling Suspension Bridge, which connects Wheeling, West Virginia, to Bridgeport, Ohio. The road slices through the state, passing through the state capital, Columbus, and moving on to Indiana. As you travel westward on the National Road through the eastern portion of the state, the Appalachian hills give way to flatter plains. There are opportunities to explore all eras of American history along this road, from the earliest settlements to the newest attractions.

Begin this journey by sneaking over the state line across the suspension bridge. Designed by J. A. Roebling, the engineer who introduced wire cabling and stiffening trusses to the suspension bridge, the Wheeling Suspension Bridge was the longest bridge in the world (at just over one thousand feet) when it was built in 1849.

To see Ohio's oldest sandstone bridge, drive eight miles west from the Wheeling Suspension Bridge to Blaine. Built in 1828 specifically for the National Road Project, the sandstone bridge fell into disrepair in the late twentieth century. U.S. 40's newer bridge towers above it, but the old S-type bridge, with its three arches, was recognized for its historical qualities—it was the first bridge constructed in Ohio and possibly in the Northwest Territory—and it was restored for Ohio's bicentennial.

The National Road soon passes through St. Clairsville, where the imposing Belmont County Courthouse is among the most eye-catching sights in town. A few miles west, the Lentz Tavern stands as a reminder of how early settlers found rest and refreshment along the road.

The Salt Fork S-Bridge is one of four S-bridges along Ohio's section of the National Road. The S-shaped bridge—Ohio's largest—curves to accommodate the angles of the river. Visit Salt Fork State Park to get a feeling for the natural history of this area, which once was covered with dense, old-growth forest. Settlers cleared the land, then found its clay ideal for pottery, and later mined its coal for industry. Morgan's Raiders, the infamous band of confederate soldiers led by cavalryman John Hunt Morgan, were chased

By restoring old canal paths and converting overgrown, now-historical rail lines into working bike paths, regions of Ohio have enjoyed a growth in tourism. Groups of bikers, families on foot, rollerbladers, and bird-watchers now converge on little towns such as Yellow Springs, Peninsula, and Newark to take advantage of a smooth walk through the rough-and-tumble Ohio countryside.

In Newark, the Licking County Recreational trail system traverses the county east to west and north to south with paths developed for cyclists and walkers. Locals know the path, but outsiders arriving for a visit can gain the best access to the trail by booking a stay at the Cherry Valley Lodge, which sits at an entrance to the trail system's first path. With the distinction of being the only hotel in the United States that's also a full-fledged arboretum, the Cherry Valley Lodge is a beautiful place to stay. Guests booked at the hotel are also welcome to hire bicycles for the day to use en route to nearby Granville—a cute little town filled with old-fashioned shops—or to take on the full twenty-eight-mile round-trip ride between the lodge and Johnstown. Known for its wildflowers in the early spring and its canopied foliage in the fall, this trail gives insight into rural Ohio's best offerings.

Since 1814, Zanesville's confluence of the Muskingum and Licking rivers has been traversed by five iterations of the Y-bridge. The first was made of wood.

The Wheeling Suspension Bridge, completed by John Roebling in 1860, is the oldest single-span suspension bridge in the world. The bridge carried the National Road across the Ohio River from Wheeling, West Virginia, to Belmont County, Ohio.

A bull bison stares down the photographer at the Wilds in Muskingum County. The Wilds is the largest research and captive-breeding facility for rare and endangered herbivores in North America.

The Belmont County Courthouse at Saint Clairsville was completed in 1885 in the Beaux Arts style. Adjoining the courthouse are an old jail and sheriff's residence.

through Salt Fork by Union troops. The present-day Salt Fork Lodge allows visitors a more restful sleep than Morgan's Raiders had.

Outside Salt Fork State Park, sections of the National Road retain their original charm. Italianate and Federal-style houses in the town of Old Washington are reminiscent of New England, while Peacock Road illustrates the brick paving used on the original National Road. Peacock is one of the best-preserved sections of the "old road."

Just before you reach New Concord, stop by the John and Annie Glenn Historic Site to hear the story of the humble-astronaut-turned-beloved-senator. The Glenns initially demurred at the thought of being immortalized in this way, but when they were promised that the center would be an educational facility depicting American history through the story of their lives, they agreed. The boyhood home of John Glenn, surrounded by a white picket fence, was built by his father. The house had to be moved when the National Road was widened, but today it stands overlooking the National Road once again, decorated as it would have been at the time it was built.

Those who traversed the National Road in its earliest days faced many predators. Bears and wildcats presented a real threat to the earliest travelers, but those travelers never encountered anything like what modern-day visitors see. Foxes, gazelles, giraffes, and rhinoceroses now inhabit the Wilds, a preserve and scientific research center that provides a habitat for exotic wildlife. Visitors can tour the park and see an amazing variety of animals, then learn about conservation at the visitor center.

The Wild West is largely the topic explored at the National Road/Zane Grey Museum. In a roundabout way, this center is dedicated to the ideas that traveled back and forth along the National Road and to the influence these ideas had on our nation's development. Zane Grey, a resident of Zanesville, voraciously ate up the stories and legends that traveled along the National Road. He published more than eighty books romanticizing the life he heard about, becoming the "father of the adult Western." It's fitting that the National Road and Grey's work are celebrated together at this museum. Memorabilia such as National Road mile markers and regional artifacts add to the ambience here.

Zanesville is home to another letter in the "bridge alphabet" that makes up the overpasses of this section of the National Road. Zanesville's Y-bridge has been through many iterations since its first construction in the early 1800s. Five separate Y-bridges have spanned the convergence of the Muskingum and Licking rivers. The bridge now standing was dedicated in 1984, and though its construction doesn't afford pretty river views, as previous designs did, the bridge does provide a memorable crossing over the two rivers.

West of Zanesville, Ohio's first mining area predates the coalfields by thousands of years. Flint Ridge State Memorial features a visitor center built around a prehistoric quarry pit where early people worked hard to mine flint for tools and weapons. The geology of the park is complemented by its beauty, and a visit here provides an education: Felling a tree with an ax is difficult; making an ax strong enough to fell a tree is an accomplishment.

Dawes Arboretum, located just east of Ohio Route 13 near Newark, also represents the ancient in Ohio. Here a prime section of old-growth forest remains untouched. More than one thousand acres of natural scenery are protected here, and visitors can either take a driving tour or walk along the property trails. Maps at the visitor center help interpret the areas of the arboretum that represent the old-growth forest and the acres dedicated to the latest in experimental agriculture.

Nothing along the National Road, however, is as striking as the hamper in Newark. Home of the Longaberger Basket Company headquarters, this basket-shaped building is eye-popping, and uninitiated travelers are often stunned to see the seven-story basket resting alongside the road (just south of Ohio Route 40 on Main Street in Newark). Visitors can tour the building and find out more about this successful local company that turned a poor family into a regional powerhouse.

The tour of the eastern portion of the National Road ends near the outskirts of Columbus.

FAIRFIELD, PICKAWAY, AND ROSS COUNTIES
BOUNTIFUL ROUTES

When the harvest starts to come in, a crop of handmade signs pops up along the roads just south of Columbus, announcing the availability of cider, corn, hay rides, homemade apple fritters, and pumpkins galore. The whole region comes alive with celebrations leading up to Halloween, particularly the area around Circleville, where the nation's biggest—and, locals would argue, the best—pumpkin celebration occurs. Farther south, mystics of every variety seem to flock to the region's many mound formations to extract ancient knowledge. Their strange rituals provide fodder for local news outlets around the time of All Souls' Day, but "regular people" come here as well, to marvel at and reflect on the ways of those cultures that were here before us.

Pickerington, Ohio, became a city in 1991. A benefactor, or victim, of urban sprawl, Pickerington had long been a sleepy dairy community until it was discovered by Columbus citizens looking for a quieter place to live. The city struggles with managing growth, but Pickerington Ponds Preserve is likely to maintain its pristine beauty for centuries to come. Known for its bird-watching opportunities, the preserve offers two observation areas ideal for spotting herons and other wading birds.

From the preserve, head south on Ohio Route 33, which takes on the characteristics of a country road the farther south you go. The city of Lancaster, laid out along the banks of the Hocking River, boasts three historic districts. The Sherman House, in downtown Lancaster, was the birthplace of both General William Sherman and his brother, Senator John Sherman (sponsor of the Sherman Antitrust Act). The house is now a museum.

Fairfield County has eighteen covered bridges, the most in the state. Four of the bridges reside on private property, but the rest make touring the county a veritable treasure hunt for varying styles and colors of the bridges.

ROUTE 13

This tour begins in Pickerington and follows U.S. Route 33 east to Lancaster. From Lancaster, follow U.S. Route 22 west to Circleville, then U.S. Route 56 east to State Route 159 west into Chillicothe. The Mound City Group National Monument is just northwest of Chillicothe on State Route 207. From Route 207, follow U.S. Route 50 west to Bainbridge.

Mist clears from the hillsides, viewed from the stubble of a cornfield near Laurelville in Hocking County.

This sturdy 1881 barn, complete with octagonal cupola and monitor roof extensions, is one of the centerpieces at Slate Run Living Historical Farm, near Lithopolis in Pickaway County.

The Mink Hollow Covered Bridge, built in 1887 over Arney Run in Fairfield County, has a fifty-three-foot multiple kingpost truss.

Columbus teems with young and determined politicos out to make a name for themselves in state politics and beyond. But drive a few minutes outside of the city and you enter a slower-paced world. Historic little towns such as Westerville, Worthington, and Delaware maintain their charm with a loving dignity, allowing visitors to easily imagine what life was like in central Ohio more than a hundred years ago.

Civil War aficionados will make Lancaster their stop of choice when touring central Ohio. The Little Brown House on the Hill, as the locals call it, was built in 1811 and is the birthplace of William Tecumseh Sherman and his brother John, a U.S. senator. Raised in this humble brick house, William would grow up to take Atlanta in the Civil War, and John would author the Sherman Antitrust Act. These days, visitors can tour the house to view Sherman family memorabilia as well as Civil War and other historical documents.

The Sherman House sits in the midst of four National Historic Districts that define the proud little town, and visitors are free to roam the city to gaze at the architecturally significant homes and commercial buildings that make this a sort of outdoor museum. The town's newest indoor attraction is the Ohio Glass Museum. Paying tribute to the region's industry, the museum provides both a tour of regional history and a celebration of craftsmanship.

General William Tecumseh Sherman, born in Lancaster, won the fiercest battles of the Civil War and was given command of the entire U.S. Army after Grant was elected president.

Individuals, corporations, and civic organizations work hard to maintain these bucolic treasures, and many of the bridges have been refurbished in recent years.

Natural beauty is a priority in Lancaster County, which is home to five state nature preserves. Christmas Rocks and Shallenberger state nature preserves feature the rock formations and rugged wilderness that define the Hocking Hills region of southeast Ohio. At Shallenberger, Allen Knob comprises 240 feet of tough sandstone and is a familiar landmark to locals. Christmas Rocks and Shallenberger deliver plenty of delights for nature fans: tulip trees, high ridges, and wildflowers, to name just a few.

Switch from Route 33 to Ohio Route 22 to head southwest to Circleville, which derived its name from the ancient circular earthworks on which the town was planned. The original earthworks were built by the Hopewell culture thousands of years ago and had a 1,100-foot diameter. Later residents disliked the circular plan, and as a result, the town became the first in the country to undergo urban redevelopment.

Modern folks think the town's name is a result of its love for the ripe, round pumpkins that are harvested in the region and celebrated at the Circleville Pumpkin Show. Since its inception in 1903, this successful festival has relied on the enthusiasm of everyone in the city. Residents call it "the greatest free show on earth" and pour an immense amount of effort into parades, exhibits, special events, and, of course, the cultivation of massive pumpkins.

The region surrounding Circleville is rich with wildlife. Stage's Pond is a thirty-acre kettle lake formed by a glacial depression. It is a favorite stop for migrating waterfowl and a nesting ground for blue herons.

North of Circleville, Slate Run Living Historical Farm preserves its buildings—and animal breeds—with pride. The Gothic Revival farmhouse on the property dates to 1856, and Amish craftsmen recently restored the farm's impressive multi-bay barn. Kids enjoy the unusual breeds of farm animals and ask the costumed interpreters plenty of questions about the Poland China hogs and merino sheep. The truly curious are put to work on the farm, helping with chores in order to get a feeling for life in the mid-1800s.

South of Circleville, the Hocking Hills begin to appear and the landscape gets more interesting. State parks and nature preserves provide opportunities for gentle walks, as well as white-water kayaking, mountain biking on rugged trails, and rock climbing on stark cliff walls.

This is the rugged country where mound builders created their mysterious ancient earthworks. The Mound City Group National Monument in Chillicothe pays tribute to the ancient Hopewells who constructed mounds in geometric patterns—sometimes with walls that were twelve feet high and mounds that were up to thirty feet high. Spanning large tracts of land, these achievements were constructed between 200 BC and AD 500 and are studied by experts who hope to determine their meaning and purpose. Plan to spend some time at the visitor center and then walk the trails to explore the mounds.

Chillicothe is also the site of Adena, the two-thousand-acre estate of Thomas Worthington, Ohio's sixth governor. Benjamin Henry Latrobe, the architect who designed the U.S. Capitol under Thomas Jefferson, designed Worthington's house; it is one of only three homes designed by Latrobe still standing in the United States. The official seal of the state of Ohio depicts a view from the property. Visitors to Adena can enjoy a tour of the home, in which many original furnishings stand, as well as a tour of the estate's recently restored gardens and additional original structures.

Southwest of Chillicothe, the town of Bainbridge is the site of the Seip Mound, a burial mound of the Hopewells that has produced evidence of highly developed craftsmanship. Visitors also flock to the Seven Caves to explore the paved and lighted walkways. But the Dr. John Harris Dental Museum provides the quirkiest—and slightly unnerving—diversion, taking a look at the art and science of dentistry. Home to the nation's first dental school, Bainbridge has been called "the cradle of American dentistry." The museum, housed in the former school, details the industry's milestones throughout the years and displays a collection of instruments and educational tools.

PART IV

SOUTHWEST OHIO
THE QUEEN CITY AND ITS SURROUNDS

FACING PAGE:
The Little Miami River tumbles through the Clifton Gorge State Nature Preserve near the village of Clifton in Greene County. During spring, dozens of wildflower species bloom among the limestone rocks of the gorge.

ABOVE:
The construction of Chateau LaRoche, also known as Loveland Castle, was begun in 1929 by recluse Harry Andrews, who continued working on the medieval castle along the Little Miami River until his death, at age ninety, in 1981.

Southern Ohio is a study in contrasts. The southeastern portion of the state is renowned for its beauty but is troubled by poverty. Only a few hundred miles away, southwestern Ohio explodes with diversity, commerce, and invention. Cincinnati was one of the nation's first great inland cities, not to mention the birthplace of the modern baseball league. In Dayton, the brothers Wright first dreamed of flying, giving wing to generations of wealth built on aerodynamics. The Ohio River has supplied endless opportunities for commerce, from the transportation of goods and people to riverboat cruising and gambling to modern industry. Some of the railroad lines that died out in the middle of the twentieth century are being reborn through this region's rails-to-trails program, giving rise to a new tourist trade, and the region's parks and natural areas entice visitors to make repeat returns.

OHIO RIVER TOWNS
A MEANDERING TOUR PAST RIVER TOWNS, FLOODPLAINS, AND MURALS

ROUTE 14

This drive follows U.S. Route 52, the Ohio River Scenic Byway, beginning at Portsmouth and heading west past Shawnee State Park, Manchester (Moyer Vineyards is well marked on the route near Manchester), and Ripley, where the Rankin House is visible from the route. Continue heading west on U.S. 52 to Point Pleasant.

U.S. Route 52 follows the Ohio River's winding path and is an easy-to-follow, scenic route for those unable to purchase a sternwheeler. Starting in Portsmouth, take a long walk alongside the city's floodwall murals. Their slogan—"2,000 years of history, 2,000 feet of art"—is catchy and true. Fifty-two panels depict life in the region, from the earliest records left by the Hopewells to the time of the murals' dedication in 2002. This massive civic project is one of the largest mural projects in the world. Wear comfortable shoes so you can continue your stroll into downtown Portsmouth and through its antique shops and small historic museums.

South of Portsmouth, Shawnee State Park is known as "the Little Smokies." Rugged and hilly, the forest in the park has one distinctive feature: a blue haze that seems to linger over it. This vapor is caused by moisture in the forest evaporating into the air. From the ridges in the park, the Shawnees could watch the slow but steady progress of white settlers, and this area served as the stage for conflict throughout the settlement era.

From Shawnee State Park, the Ohio River meanders south, passing by small river towns, each with its own personality. The region between Cincinnati and Ripley is known for two crops, wine and tobacco. Vintner Nicholas Longworth, known as the "father of American winemaking," planted thousands of acres of vineyards along the shores of the Ohio River in the early 1800s. Longworth won awards in Europe for the casks he produced here, but vine diseases and the Civil War destroyed his vineyards. In the 1970s, wine scholars revisited Longworth's original vision and planted vineyards again. A cottage industry flourished, and today the Nicholas Longworth Heritage Wine Trail celebrates the state's original vintner. The Moyer Vineyards Winery in Manchester is known for its champagne and gourmet dining. Visitors can enjoy Ohio River views while sampling wines.

Southwest

Sturdy houses line the banks of the Ohio River at Ripley, in Brown County. Ohio's only burley tobacco auctions are held annually in this town on the Ohio River Scenic Byway.

Visitors gain a bird's-eye view of Ripley and the Ohio River from the Rankin House, which was used as a stop on the Underground Railroad in the early 1800s.

This humble home on a hilltop in Ripley was a homecoming and a symbol of freedom for slaves who made the journey safely across the Ohio River, under cover of night, and up the steps leading to the Rankin House.

Head from one vice to another: The town of Ripley is home to Ohio's last tobacco market. With three large tobacco warehouses in town, anyone trying to shake the habit might want to pass straight through town without stopping. Head west through the countryside toward Cincinnati and you'll have good opportunities to see old Mail Pouch Tobacco barns.

As the tobacco trade becomes less popular, Ripley is marketing its other significant attractions, most notably its role in the Underground Railroad. Ripley's Rankin House is one of the better-known stops on the Underground Railroad. And with the construction of the National Underground Railroad Freedom Center in Cincinnati, the Rankin House—and the town of Ripley—is enjoying a new surge of visitors. The result of a fortunate combination of strategic locale and humanitarian homeowner, the house provided refuge for some two thousand slaves who made the final and most dangerous journey across the Ohio River from Kentucky. From the Rankin House, seven bends of the Ohio River can be seen. One hundred steps ascend from the riverbank to the house, and the Rankin family proudly noted that they never lost a passenger.

Born in a three-room house along the banks of the Ohio River, Ulysses S. Grant put Point Pleasant, Ohio, on the map. While many are aware that Grant toured the countryside during his life, few people realize that his boyhood home did, too. His little Point Pleasant house was put on a barge and toured around the country. It was then positioned in Columbus on the Ohio State Fairgrounds before making its way back to its original locale in 1927. Open for tours from April to October, the home is the shining memorial in the little, unincorporated town of Point Pleasant.

LITTLE MIAMI TOUR
STAGECOACH STOPS, ANCIENT HISTORY, AND NATURAL BEAUTY

So many of Ohio's small-town routes began as American Indian trails, canal lines, or railways, but the area around the Little Miami River enjoys a romantic stagecoach background. What is now U.S. Route 42 once bore the scars of wooden wagon wheels from the Accommodation Line stagecoach that carried passengers along this route. Now U.S. Route 22 and U.S. Route 42 provide scenic alternatives to nearby Interstate 71 for those who want to drive this route, but if there's a bike rack on your car, consider bringing along your bicycle. A bike path—the Little Miami National and State Scenic River and Trail—follows the river, almost on its banks, from Loveland all the way up to Cedar Creek State Park. The river can also be experienced from a canoe, and canoe liveries along the way accommodate sightseers with affordable rates and easy-to-follow routes.

From Loveland northward, the terrain delivers a host of opportunities for recreation, ranging from roller coasters to state parks to antique shopping. Plan to spend a long day exploring this portion of southwest Ohio.

Just before Valentine's Day, the post office in Loveland, where this tour begins, welcomes a host of senior-citizen volunteers, who hand-cancel more than twenty thousand valentines seeking the "Loveland, Ohio" stamp of approval. A cupid cachet and love verse on the letter make a nice touch for lovers who go out of their way to forward their cards to the postmaster in this town.

The only city in the state to straddle three counties, Loveland enjoyed a recent gentrification—streets paved with bricks and walks lined with park benches. Loveland's castle, Chateau Laroche, was the lifelong project of local eccentric and World War I veteran Harry Andrews. Flattening fields, digging drainage ditches and even a moat, and dragging fieldstones to the building site, Andrews built himself a proper knight's castle. He died in his nineties, having accomplished almost all of the work on this castle by himself, and willed his property to the youths of the area. Andrews had long been a

ROUTE 15

Begin this tour in Loveland. Take Interstate 71 north to Kings Mills and Kings Island. Continue north on State Route 15, then take State Route 48 north to Lebanon, then follow U.S. Route 42 north toward Waynesville. Head east to State Route 73 to visit Caesar Creek State Park. Return to Route 42, heading north through Xenia, then continue on State Route 72 north to John Bryan State Park.

American sycamore trees straddle the bank along Caesar Creek, a tributary of the Little Miami River in Warren County.

Fort Ancient Trading Post, a haven for local antique collectors, sits high on a bluff above the west bank of the Little Miami River near Fort Ancient, an earthworks built by Hopewells two thousand years ago.

More than three million Christmas lights festoon Clifton Mill and the banks of the Little Miami River gorge during the holiday season. A collection of more than three thousand Santas adds to the yuletide fun.

Ohio's transition from an agricultural economy to a steel and manufacturing economy can be illustrated by its bridges. Here, a steel bridge spans the Little Miami River where a charming covered bridge might have in the past.

volunteer with local youth groups; he dubbed his young friends the "Knights of the Golden Trail." Visitors can peer into the odd life that Andrews led, from a visit to the fortified dungeon to a look at the castle's special throne: a toilet made of stone bricks.

Royalty of a different kind thrives in Kings Mills, originally a company town for the King's Great Western Powder Company and the Peters Cartridge Company. Gunpowder and shells went together like bacon and eggs, and the town thrived during the late 1800s. Powder production continued here through World War II. After the war, the property was sold to the Taft Broadcasting Company for the creation of Kings Island, an amusement

GATEWAY TO FREEDOM

With the opening of the National Underground Railroad Freedom Center, many of the historical sites related to the Underground Railroad in the area surrounding Cincinnati have enjoyed renewed interest. Representing the first real step toward freedom for slaves strong enough to cross the Ohio River under cover of night, the Cincinnati region was a main thoroughfare along the route to safety. Historical markers and monuments announce the churches and sites in the region that gave refuge to the slaves, but touring the safe houses that operated in the mid-1800s provides the best understanding of everyone involved in the story—the

slaves who sought refuge and the families who risked everything to provide that refuge.

The Rankin House in Ripley, with its stone steps leading up from the Ohio River, serves as one of the region's most notable homes. But Ripley is also the site of the John P. Parker house. Parker was a slave himself who escaped and built a successful business in Ripley. He returned to Kentucky time and again to help slaves cross the river safely. In Springboro, Quaker Jonathan Wright campaigned against slavery from his home. Now a bed and breakfast, the Wright home offers tours to those not staying overnight.

park now operated by Paramount Parks (of Paramount Pictures fame) that features more than eighty rides, attractions, and shows.

While Kings Island operates some of the region's newest attractions, the city of Lebanon is home to some of the state's oldest. The town attracted Shaker settlers, and their influence is still found here in the many antique and furniture stores selling Shaker-style designs. The stores makes great stops for those who want to troll for antiques, but to get a real flavor of the truly old, visit the Golden Lamb, Ohio's oldest continuously operating inn and restaurant. Lebanon's location on the north-south route between Toledo and Cincinnati and its position near the National Road made the Golden Lamb a popular stop for travelers. The inn has welcomed travelers with names like William Webster, William Henry Harrison, and Charles Dickens. Dickens, who arrived by stagecoach, was refused a drink in the inn, which at the time observed temperance. Dickens may not have been a happy customer, but thousands of contented visitors have rested their heads at the inn since it opened in 1803. From its façade of handmade bricks to its collection of antiques, including many original Shaker pieces and an impressive collection of Currier and Ives prints, the inn offers visitors a wonderful education in history along with a tasty meal and a good night's sleep.

Along U.S. 42, the columns and balustrades of Glendower Mansion stand proudly on a hill just outside Lebanon. Originally built by John Milton Williams, one of the framers of Ohio's state constitution, the restored home is open for tours from June through August.

North of the classic columns of Glendower, ancient people used animal bones and handmade baskets to construct 18,000 feet of earthen walls used, in part, as a calendar system two thousand years ago. The Fort Ancient Interpretive Center uses the earthen walls as a starting point to tell the story of 15,000 years of American Indian history in the region.

North of Fort Ancient, Caesar Creek rivals the Little Miami River for beauty and scenery. Caesar Creek is named for a slave, originally captured by Shawnees on a raid, who was later given hunting rights to the area and who joined the Shawnees in their fight for freedom. The state park encircling Caesar Creek features Ohio's oldest sheets of exposed rock. Fossils embedded in the rock throughout the park remind visitors that the region was once covered with ocean waters. The rocks, ravines, and clear blue waters of Caesar Creek Reservoir offer some of the prettiest views in the state and create a playground of opportunities for outdoor enthusiasts.

Focusing on the specific period of southwestern Ohio history from 1793 to 1812, Caesar Creek Pioneer Village preserves the region's historic log cabins. The cabins evoke a sense of romanticism, but walk inside and consider surviving a winter with your family within four walls like these, and you'll get a better feeling for just how much hardship these early settlers endured.

This is the territory General "Mad" Anthony Wayne fought for, and the Treaty of Greenville was signed just north of here, so it's fitting that when the town of Waynesville was founded in 1797, it was named for this local hero. Today, more than seventy antique stores open their doors each morning in the

The Moore's Memorial Chapel was built at Blue Creek in Adams County in 1800, on the original site of Ohio's first Methodist church.

RIGHT PAGE: *Cedar Falls cascades over dolomite limestone rocks in Cedar Creek, near the village of Cedar Mills in Adams County. Arborvitae grows alongside rare shrubs and plants in the rugged gorge, which is managed by the Ohio chapter of The Nature Conservancy.*

historic downtown district. Architecture buffs enjoy this pedestrian-friendly city for its many historical buildings, particularly along Old Main Street.

Be certain to take in the two miles of scenery along the headwaters of the Little Miami at Clifton Gorge State Nature Preserve, and the trails at the adjacent John Bryan State Park. Remnants of the area's historical stagecoach trails now serve as paths for hikers and give an indication of just how rural a stagecoach trip could be. The real attraction here, though, is Clifton Gorge, a dramatic geological sculpture created by water on rock. Cliffs that have lost their battle with gravity overhang the pathways leading to the beautiful waterfalls of the gorge.

Just east of the park, the powerful waters of the Little Miami feed Clifton Mill. In many ways, Clifton is the "painted lady" of Ohio's mills. It is one of the largest water-powered gristmills still in existence, and is the only mill left standing on a river that once relied on a series of mills for its commerce. The mill is five stories high and, with its bright red paint, serves as a beacon to summer visitors. In winter, more than 3 million holiday lights cover the property from top to bottom. The excess doesn't stop there. The mill breaks out its collection of more than three thousand Santa Claus figures and creates a festive aura contagious to anyone seeking a look at the lights, a meal at the mill's restaurant, or a walk through its shop.

ADAMS COUNTY
OHIO'S BLUEGRASS REGION

ROUTE 16

This route follows State Route 41 south from Peebles to West Union.

Kentucky isn't the only state in the union that lays claim to Bluegrass Country. Ohio's Adams County has its share of bluegrass too; the bluegrass prairie reaches to the very edge of the Appalachian hills on the county's eastern side, giving the eye plenty to take in during a drive through this rural area. High summer is the best time to visit, when the prairie grasses are in full bloom and the Amish-tilled fields are thick with crop. The area's international attraction is the Serpent Mound, an amazing earthwork in the shape of a snake, but visitors stay in the area to hike, bike, or float their way around, or they browse through shops filled with local Amish crafts.

Begin your tour at the Serpent Mound in Peebles. Depicting a serpent with seven distinctive coils about to devour an egg, this quarter-mile-long effigy has provoked great speculation within the scientific, archeological, and mystic communities. Though it most resembles a snake, some believe it was constructed by either the Hopewell or Fort Ancient culture in response to comets in the night sky. (Recently, hot debate among scientists has arisen over which culture was responsible for building the mounds.) Some believe it was used as a landmark for spaceships. All agree that it was not a burial ground and that it is the largest such effigy in the United States.

Adams Lake State Park and the Edge of Appalachia Preserve showcase the prairie grasses that have made the region a favorite of conservationists. An abundance of plant life attracts songbirds here, and visitors who walk through the parks are trekking through one of the most biologically diverse areas of the Midwest.

For a bird's-eye view of the area, tackle the trailhead to Buzzardroost Rock at the Christian and Emmet Goetz Nature Preserve. A moderate three-mile climb up Buzzardroost will take you more than three hundred feet above the Brush Creek Valley and closer to the birds that nest on the cliffs.

In the town of West Union, a Mennonite community thrives alongside a pocket of Cincinnatians and Daytonians who left the urban center for these quiet hills. The Murphin Ridge Inn, owned by former urbanites, offers guests their choice of a private cabin or a room in the inn, and plenty of good cooking. (Reserve a table in advance, this is one of the best eateries in the county and they book up quickly on weekends.) The inn's office and four dining rooms are housed in an 1828 brick farmhouse that features an extension constructed with logs from a circa-1803 cabin. It serves as an inviting welcome to the inn experience. The main inn, recently constructed, resembles a large barn. Nine cabins are set apart from the main property, and a fire pit gives guests a chance to commune under the night sky.

Just a short walk or drive from the inn, a series of Amish stores sell everything from bulk foods to hot cross buns to bunk beds. Farms in and around the area sport signs advertising fresh eggs or handmade quilts, and during fall, signs appear touting pumpkins and gourds for sale.

West Union also maintains a 63-foot-long covered bridge. Though it's no longer in use, the Kirker Bridge, built in 1890, can be seen from Ohio Route 41.

OXFORD AREA TOUR
THE "YALE OF THE WEST"

Settlers eager to develop a higher education center in the Northwest Territory established Oxford, Ohio, in 1809 as the "Yale of the West." Miami University was the result of their efforts, and the school has maintained its commitment to scholarship ever since. This tour begins in Oxford, extends to Hueston Woods, and circles back to the Indian Creek Preserve Metroparks, winding up in the town of Hamilton.

The Miami University campus feels like an Eastern coastal town. Buildings such as Upham Hall, with its central archway and bell tower, lend the campus an old-school feel and are the stuff of legend—kiss your sweetheart under the arch at midnight and you'll soon be married. The Beta Bell Tower is a campus landmark, as is the dome of the building that houses

ROUTE 17
Begin this tour at Hueston Woods State Park, then head south on State Route 732 toward Oxford. Turn right at Hamilton Scipio Road, then take a sharp left onto Cincinnati Brookville Road, then a right on Bebb Park Lane to visit Governor Bebb Preserve. Return to Route 129 and head east into Hamilton.

Dogwoods brighten the walkways at Miami University, which poet Robert Frost once stated had "the prettiest campus that ever was."

The Governor Bebb Pioneer Village in Butler County is named for Ohio's nineteenth governor, William Bebb, who was born in 1799 in a log cabin that now serves as the centerpiece of the Pioneer Village.

Daniel Boone's cousin Thomas and members of his family are buried at the Indian Creek Pioneer Church and Burial Ground in the village of Reily in Butler County.

THE ICE CREAM TRAIL

Debate has raged over the years about the origin of the banana split. Latrobe, Pennsylvania (more famous for its Rolling Rock beer), lays claim to inventing the concoction, as does Boston. But in Wilmington, Ohio, they'll hear nothing of it. It is here, they say, that local Ernest Hazard developed the treat in the early 1900s. And only in Wilmington will you find a celebration of the treat at the town's annual Banana Split Festival, which takes place every June.

Ice cream enthusiasts who miss the June event can travel north out of Wilmington and pass through Xenia on to the town of Yellow Springs, where Young's Jersey Dairy dominates the local scene. Young's farm started in the 1860s, but it wasn't until a hundred years later that the family started selling ice cream. These days, families arrive at the "farm" to do everything from playing a round of putt-putt golf to taking a swing in the batting cages and, of course, having a scoop or two of the family's famous ice cream.

the architecture department, Alumni Hall. An outdoor sculpture park and art museum are two don't-miss visitor attractions on campus.

In downtown Oxford, pick up a copy of the walking-tour brochure from the visitor center. More than one hundred historically and architecturally significant homes and businesses are housed in a twelve-block radius here. The downtown area is lively with college kids and university types, and the stores reflect their needs: bookstores, art galleries, coffee shops, and gift shops.

Take College Corner Pike north out of town to Todd Road and drive to Hueston Woods State Park. With 200 acres of old-growth forest; fishing and boating on Acton Lake; and 150 species of birds flitting about, the park has all the traditional amenities you expect. But it also has some lively diversions that cater to the university crowd: an eighteen-hole golf course and a paintball course, where students can blow off steam. The park also hosts fossil hunts.

The campus of Miami University in Oxford testifies to the state's early commitment to higher education. The school was envisioned in 1803, when the city had hardly any residents. This panoramic photo was taken in 1909. Now, more than 14,000 students converge on the campus each year.

A lodge, cottages, and campsites provide options for overnight guests, and special campsites for equestrians are available too.

The roads from Hueston Woods to Okeana (south of Oxford) are dotted with interesting sites belonging to the Butler County Metroparks system. The Indian Creek Pioneer Church and Burial Ground was the first official burial ground in the area. The cemetery dates back to 1810, and the church was built in 1829. Indian Creek Preserve features a hiking trail that leads to an ancient mound, and the Bunker Hill Pioneer Universalist Cemetery is the final resting place for soldiers from the Revolutionary War, the War of 1812, the Mexican-American War, and the Civil War. The Bressler brothers, who fought on opposite sides during the War Between the States, are buried here.

The final park along this stretch of road passes under two covered bridges at the entrance to the Governor Bebb Preserve and Wildlife Village. The centerpiece of the park is the log cabin in which Bebb, the nineteenth governor of Ohio, was born.

As you travel eastward, the county seat of Hamilton offers a host of interesting sites and markers. The Mosler Safe Company seems to have a lock on the town. It built the vault that protects the Declaration of Independence, the Bill of Rights, and the Constitution. Mosler is also responsible for engineering the vault at Fort Knox. The inventor of the Richter scale was born here too.

Hamilton is also home to an octagon house that was built, complete with spiral staircase, in 1863. It's open for tours on weekdays. Downtown, Monument Cabin is also open for tours. More recently, the city invested a great deal of effort into a public sculpture program, and more than thirty pieces are now installed throughout town. That number rises to more than 130 sculptures during the town's annual ice sculpture festival in January.

SOUTHEAST OHIO
A LITTLE APPALACHIA

Water cascades ninety feet over the lip of Ash Cave, a sandstone proscenium in Hocking Hills State Park. In severe winters, the entire waterfall freezes, forming an ice cone.

This weather-beaten Appalachian crib barn stands in a field near Amesville in rural Athens County.

The southeastern portion of the state is blessed with natural beauty. The Hocking Hills region—Appalachia's foothills—celebrates natural treasures and historical landmarks. In recent history, a great deal of sweat equity has been invested into the tourism trade. This grassroots movement has greatly benefited the region, increasing interest and generating much-needed revenue for the people who live and work here. A cottage industry—of cottages—has sprung up as visitors discover the area's rural charm.

Rock shelters, cliffs, gorges, forested land, rivers, and hills lend the region a visual appeal, and the area's natural beauty is protected by a series of nature preserves, state parks, and state forests. The numerous parks are a treasure to those who live close enough to take full advantage of all of the outdoor recreational opportunities; the parks make a surprising "find" for the growing number of out-of-town visitors who are beginning to discover the area.

The town of Athens, home to Ohio University, has long maintained its collegiate charm and fostered a gentle quirkiness that encourages and supports some of the area's more unusual businesses. Many artists and craftspeople choose to live and work in this area, giving each stop along the way a dose of individuality.

River culture takes over along the southeastern edge of Ohio, and the Covered Bridge Scenic Byway guides drivers across a healthy series of historical bridges to sites that celebrate Ohio's past. This 35-mile route includes sites rich with history, French influence, and religious significance.

The far eastern portion of the river has much to share with neighboring West Virginia. The coal industry plays a role here, and stories of fortunes made and lost are told along the riverbanks at places like Blennerhassett Island. Bob Evans's empire began here, and conservationists work hard to maintain the forgotten past of the furnace industry that once thrived in this region.

One of the region's best-kept secrets is its roads. They wind, dip, twist, and turn, creating a roller-coaster ride for drivers who enjoy a challenge. It is rumored that the Hocking Hills region is a favorite spot for professional test-drivers and auto reviewers, and the blacktop curves have served as featured locales in national car ads. For those who like to drive, this region is Ohio's most fun.

The region's very best resource, though, is its people. Business owners depend on tourism, and they make you feel welcome wherever you go. Stay overnight, eat in a diner, shop at a local store, and you'll really feel like you're contributing to the health of the place.

HOCKING HILLS, VINTON COUNTY, AND JACKSON COUNTY
THE LONG AND WINDING ROAD

ROUTE 18

Begin this tour in Logan and follow U.S. Route 33 east to Nelsonville and Athens.

Logan provides an excellent launching point for a tour of the Hocking Hills region. In the center of a series of forests, nature preserves, and parks, this town along Lake Logan is accessible by U.S. Route 33, which is a state scenic byway that cuts through the region. But veer off onto the backroads that

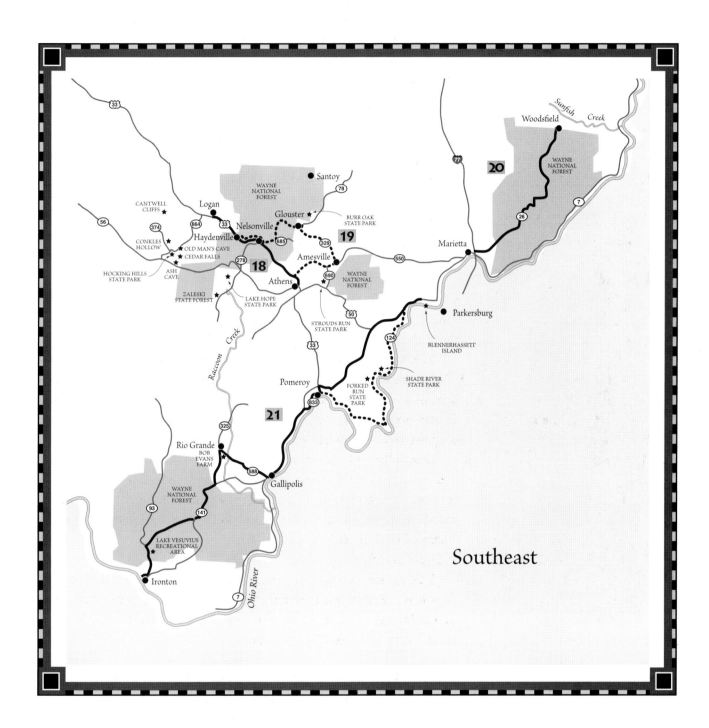

The mural adorning this old barn along State Route 180 in Hocking County testifies to an earlier age when chewing tobacco was a socially acceptable form of relaxation. A barn painter employed by the tobacco company would paint the barn at no cost to the owner, in return for displaying the mural.

The Rim Trail at Conkle's Hollow State Nature Preserve in the Hocking Hills offers one of the most scenic hikes in Ohio, with fine views of fall color from sandstone cliffs more than 150 feet tall.

The old Hope Furnace near Lake Hope once attracted industrious workers; now it's a reward for hikers who take to the trails surrounding Lake Hope State Park and Zaleski State Forest.

Located directly below the opening to a cave, Rock House—and the stone bridge that leads to it—was once used by robbers and horse thieves as a hideout. The trail of thieves is now cleaned up and a forested path leads to Rock House's front door, but the bridge is slated for replacement in 2007.

Stone Bridge, Rock House.
Hocking Co. Ohio.

wind through the forests and state parks if you really want to get a taste of the place.

One of Logan's most interesting businesses is Garden Accents. Specializing in garden products produced by the Logan Clay Products Company, this outlet store offers garden ceramics ranging from small tiles to oversized pedestals, all made from clay mined in the region. In operation since 1890, Logan Clay's Old Kiln Number 19 has been transformed into a showroom displaying an amazing compendium of products.

Ohio Route 664 north of Logan leads to Rockbridge State Nature Preserve. A one-hundred-foot-long rock bridge arches fifty feet above a ravine. The state's largest natural bridge (there are eleven others) can be accessed by taking one of two loop trails in the park; the second loop trail leads to a rock shelter of similar beauty.

South on U.S. 664, Hocking Hills State Park is home to more noteworthy geological sites. This popular park is typically populated with visitors who come to see Ash Cave, Old Man's Cave, and Cantwell Cliffs. These recess caves are fairly easy to access by trails, which lead along the ridge lines or through the gorges. Along the way, hemlock trees, waterfalls, and dramatic cliffs keep the routes interesting. A more challenging and remote trail along Queer Creek leads through narrow crevices to Cedar Falls, the region's most voluminous falls.

Cedar Falls is also the namesake of a favorite local hostel, the Inn at Cedar Falls. Nestled just near the falls on a beautiful stretch of land, the inn's original cabin now serves as the entranceway to a larger complex that features a barn converted into an inn, a series of private cabins, and a wonderful restaurant.

On hot summer days, Conkle's Hollow is a favorite destination for those trying to escape the heat. The deepest gorge in Ohio, many sections of the valley floor don't see the sunlight because of the trees; hemlocks and birches tower overhead. The deeper into the gorge you hike, the narrower it becomes, until there is only three hundred feet from sheer cliff to sheer cliff on either side.

Just west of Hocking Hills State Park, Wayne National Forest is one of the few places in the area where rock climbers and rappellers can pursue their passion. It is also a fine example of sustained multiple use. Some of the old-growth trees preserved here are four hundred to five hundred years old, but others are harvested under the watchful eye of the state forest agency.

Just to the east of the forest, Lake Hope State Park is an excellent example of Ohio's second-growth forest. Like much of the forestland in the state, the trees surrounding Lake Hope were once cut down to accommodate industry. At Lake Hope, it was the smelting industry that killed the forest, but over the last hundred years or so, oak and hickory trees have experienced a rebirth, and their renewed health has brought back flora and fauna. Lake Hope is a favorite destination of orchid fans who come in search of the elusive yellow lady's slipper. Lake Hope and its tributaries also make a fine home for Ohio's rebounding beaver population, which are a source of entertainment for the

Workers at the Buckeye Iron Furnace in Jackson County were often paid in "scrip," which they could exchange for goods and services at this company store.

The diminutive dwarf crested iris is found in April and May along roadsides in southern Ohio.

Mist rises from the hillsides at Conkle's Hollow State Nature Preserve in the Hocking Hills.

visitors who discover them. Lake Hope offers a lodge and cabins, and the shores of the lake welcome swimmers and boaters in the warm seasons.

A hundred years ago, the Hocking Hills region was often referred to as the Hanging Rock Iron Region. Evidence of the old industry exists in the furnaces that operated here; the Buckeye Furnace, Union Furnace, and Hope Furnace are now state memorials to the industry that cleared the forest. In Zaleski State Forest, full-grown trees now shade the Hope Furnace. In its heyday, it burned timber twenty-four hours a day, consuming all the trees that surrounded it for miles. Visitors can still pick up the "slag" that surrounds the furnace, which now stands as a testimony to man's dominance over nature; the trees that have grown up around the furnace, however, testify even more loudly to nature's dominance over man.

The brave of heart travel deeper into the Zaleski State Forest for a look at Raccoon Creek and an "I-dare-you" session at the opening of the storied Moonville Tunnel. The tunnel was built to accommodate the rail lines that crossed the area for the coal industry. The death of a brakeman who worked for the Marietta and Cincinnati Railroad triggered rumors that persist today about a ghost or a series of ghosts. The tunnel is creepy, and it's easy to see the attraction for college kids who hike up here and dare each other to walk through it. Ghosts spotted here range from a figure in white carrying a lantern to a young woman trying to find her lover. Arrive by day and leave before dusk for a safer visit.

The Hocking Hills Welcome Center, one of the best visitor centers in the state, is located just south of the intersection of U.S. 33 and Route 664. Volunteers are delighted to help plan a visit or to provide maps for specialized driving tours. The Waterfalls and Wildflower tour is a local favorite. For those exploring the region's arts and crafts, the folks at the visitor center can assist with routes leading to some of the area's off-the-beaten-path stores and artisan studios.

ATHENS AREA TOUR
COLLEGE TOWNS AND SCENIC HILLS

ROUTE 19

Begin this tour in Athens and follow State Route 550 east into Amesville. From Amesville, take State Route 329 north and then State Route 13 north to Glouster, then follow State Route 78 west into Nelsonville. Continue on U.S. 33 west into Haydenville.

The southern portion of the Hocking Hills region is home to Ohio University and a host of businesses that cater to students and university employees. Tour the area by car, or hop on the Hocking Valley Scenic Railway. Either way, you'll get a flavor of the hilly region—on twisting roads by car, or on straight and narrow tracks in a vintage locomotive. The hallmark cliffs and gorges of the Hocking Hills are celebrated at local state parks, and the culture that emerged from the hills is displayed at local museums. This area attracts residents who care deeply about their art, craft, or vocation, and they work tirelessly to build just the right kind of gallery space or business where they can showcase their life's work.

Perhaps this tradition of stick-to-itiveness began with the inception of Ohio University. Located in the area where U.S. Route 33 meets the Hocking River, Ohio University began in 1808 with a mandate from back East to offer

Ohio University enjoyed only a handful of students when it opened in 1808. This photo was taken in 1914. Famous graduates include Fox News head Rodger Ailes and newsman Matt Lauer.

an institution of higher learning to the region's new settlers. The university began with three students; it now boasts 20,000. Ohio University was the first higher education facility in the Northwest Territory. Now known as a top party school, Ohio University is best avoided around Halloween, when the streets are overrun by costumed coeds who, quite often, have had a bit too much to drink. Any other time of the year, though, Athens' old-time collegiate charm is hard to resist, and a walk through campus or along downtown streets is a refreshing journey through a scholarly atmosphere.

Brick-lined streets and meandering sidewalks pave the campus walkways, leading past a wealth of historical structures. Trisolini Gallery houses an art collection, as does the Kennedy Museum in Lin Hall. Located in the Ridges section of campus, Lin Hall used to be part of the Athens Mental Health Center, an asylum.

Cross the Hocking River for a visit to one of Athens' coziest treasures, the Dairy Barn. Under a slate roof and three cupolas, this 6,500-square-foot gallery space features some of the world's most interesting and intricately designed award-winning quilts. The barn, originally built in 1914, was saved from destruction in the 1970s by two arts enthusiasts. The Dairy Barn is now

A BIT OF WALDEN POND AT RAVEN ROCKS

Strip-mining is big business in southeast Ohio, and its effects can be seen on the landscape throughout the area—but not at Raven Rocks near Bealsville. This landscape clustered with ravines, including the dramatic Raven Rocks ravine, which holds mystical qualities ancient and modern.

Used by American Indians as a spiritual gathering place, the site was saved from miners' implements in 1970 when a group of Quakers bought the land. Ever since, the group has financed the land by growing and harvesting Christmas trees and has nurtured alternative energies, including solar power, wind power, and even hydrogen in order to prove that you can not only save a space, you can nurture, foster, and develop it smartly.

The spire of the Galbreath Memorial Chapel is framed by the branches of a giant American sycamore on the campus of Ohio University in Athens. The chapel was built in 1957 in the Modern Colonial Revival style.

Muralist Terry Fortcamp painted this historical scene on a building wall at Glouster in Athens County, one of a dozen murals painted in several southeast Ohio counties as part of a Rural Action Community Mural program.

Bricks manufactured in nearby Nelsonville were used to construct these brick kilns located alongside State Route 278 west of town.

home to the Quilt National and the Bead National. Exhibits throughout the year celebrate quilting and beadwork, as well as regional and traditional folk arts and crafts.

Next, head to Stroud Run State Park, just east of Athens on U.S. Route 50. The park features rugged ravines, the sounds of woodpeckers, and a scenic lake.

This rich land is the setting for Glasshouse Works, a treasure trove of rare and unusual plants. Serving as a sort of mecca for gardening enthusiasts, particularly those in search of rare plants and flowers, this gallery of fauna can keep a green thumb busy for hours. Tropical plants flourish here alongside trees and shrubs for the garden and home. In addition to rare plants, the Glasshouse features all things garden-related, from stone accoutrements to stained glass, along with fine art from local and nonresident craftspeople.

Earlier exotica found its way to nearby Amesville, home to the region's first library. Books were purchased with animal skins (mostly donated by raccoons) and were collected by townspeople with the goal of a library in mind. As a result, the establishment, which began circulating texts in 1804, has always been called the Coonskin Library. Amesville students introduced the town to murals, which reveal a passion for the town's history as well as a sense of humor. The murals depict troubles Amesville has had with the floodwaters of Federal Creek; the town's proud history as a stop along the Underground Railroad; and even a raccoon reading a book by the moonlight.

Loop back toward the historic town of Nelsonville for a visit to a small art-filled community. In recent years, Nelsonville has seen an explosion of galleries that celebrate regional artisans and collections from as far away as Africa. There is a decidedly youthful enthusiasm in downtown Nelsonville, particularly during art-walk weekends or on weekend nights when the galleries stay open late.

Outdoor enthusiasts shouldn't miss the opportunity to shop at the Rocky Outdoor Gear Outlet Store in downtown Nelsonville. Rocky doesn't ship product, so the store attracts visitors from throughout the region who come here to personally purchase rugged footwear for hiking and climbing, tents, and other gear.

Things weren't always this cosmopolitan in Nelsonville. The cabins at Robbins Crossing reveal just how primitive life was before the artists moved in. Cabins and buildings from the mid-1800s are open to visitors, showcasing early American antiques and treasures used by the pioneers. Robbins Crossing's General Store sells handmade crafts by local artisans; the dolls available for purchase are particularly lovely treasures.

Robbins Crossing is located on the campus of Hocking College, a technical school that has programs for restaurant and hospitality management as well as forestry and natural resources management. The campus hosts a Paul Bunyan Show every October, at which students get to show off what they're learning and to compete for "strongest," "most agile," and "best" in various lumberjacking categories.

Nelsonville was once a center for brick making, and the town's old brick kilns recently received a face-lift with the help of Hocking College and Ohio University students, who restored the three kilns using volunteer labor.

The train depot for the Hocking Valley Scenic Railway looks like something right out of an old Western. This is where passengers buy tickets and hop on board for romantic tours of the Hocking Hills. The railroad features rides on diesel and steam locomotives. The facility also restores and maintains passenger cars, cabooses, and even an old snowplow engine. Though the trains maintain a timeless charm, they do sport different themes throughout the seasons, and passengers can enjoy Easter bunny and Santa rides as well as themed journeys from spring wildflowers to autumn color.

The town of Haydenville is a curiosity in this part of the state. The National Register of Historic Places protects 121 of its structures, most of which are built from the bricks manufactured here. The entire town has a spirit of architectural sameness—apart from a select few architectural oddities such as the round house, built in the round to resemble a section of brick pipe. The Haydenville United Methodist Church features more town brick, and even piping in its eaves.

Round out this driving tour with a visit to Burr Oak State Park, stopping in the town of Glouster for a look at its mural project. Thirty panels make up this project, which celebrates the people of the town. Created at the turn of this millennium, it's one of the newest works of public art in the region.

While the ridges, valley, and pretty lake are attractions at Burr Oak, the history of the town of Santoy, which stood here until its nineteen residents voted to disband in 1931, still gets people talking. Home to the type of shootout that would become the cliché of the Western genre, Santoy suffered from equally hackneyed bandit robberies and mining-town strife. Though Burr Oak operates an up-to-date resort, it's much more fun to hire out one of its campsites. Bring along an old Zane Grey novel to read by the campfire.

COVERED BRIDGE SCENIC BYWAY
UNDER THE SHADE OF HISTORIC BEAUTY

Wayne National Forest is home to the Covered Bridge Scenic Byway. The only national forest in Ohio, Wayne features three hundred miles of trails. This section of the forest (Wayne covers three distinctive areas on Ohio's map) is defined by the Little Muskingum River that runs through it. Much of the land in the forest is privately owned, but it is protected under regulations mandated by the Forest Service, leaving a pristine wilderness that mingles with private ownership. The people who live here are proud of their status as "keepers of the forest" and maintain their treasure in concert with the guidelines set out for them.

Since the time of their construction, the national forest's four covered bridges have enjoyed a reputation as the darlings of the area. Local lore dictates that if you make a wish and then hold your breath through the entirety of the journey through a covered bridge, your wish will come true.

ROUTE 20

Begin in Marietta, then take State Route 7 east and fork onto State Route 26 heading northbound, where the Covered Bridge Scenic Byway begins. Follow State Route 26 for fifteen miles.

Harley Warwick painted more than 25,000 Mail Pouch barns in his fifty-year career as a barn painter. This barn is near State Route 26 east of Marietta.

Rolla Merydith of Marietta built the Hune Covered Bridge over the Little Muskingum River in Washington County in 1879. The stone for the bridge abutments and the yellow poplar used to make the trusses were obtained from the nearby Hune family farm.

The Knowlton Bridge in Monroe County is a three-span, 192-foot multiple kingpost truss built over the Little Muskingum River in 1887. The hills of Monroe County are often called the Switzerland of Ohio.

A team of oxen pulls a covered wagon past an earthen mound, constructed by an ancient culture thousands of years ago, near Marietta.

Isaac Rinard founded his mill in this town that was named after him. In recent history, a millstone was found in the river and was ceremoniously laid on Rinard's grave to honor him.

If you're wishing for a beautiful drive, you won't be disappointed. This is also one of the best spots in the state to see old Mail Pouch Tobacco barns, which remain some of the most enduring examples of the country's first oversized billboard campaigns.

Entering Wayne State Forest from the north via Ohio Route 26, you'll cross Sunfish Creek. Visit the Lamping Homestead Park just south of the creek. The field—cleared by the Lamping family, early homesteaders in the area—stands as testimony to the hard labor put forth by settlers to carve a life out of the land.

Continue driving on Route 26 and you'll find the turnoff to the Knowlton Bridge. At 192 feet long, it's the second-longest covered bridge in Ohio. Maintaining a great deal of its original character, the bridge sports a red roof and has endured years of floods and bad weather.

The Rinard Covered Bridge was not so lucky. It was destroyed in the floods of 2004, and local efforts are continuing to try to bring it back to its original state.

Continuing south, you'll get a good flavor of life here in the mid-1800s as you tour the General Store, the Hune House, and even an old oil well.

Marietta is one of Ohio's most beautiful cities, especially in the spring, when dogwoods, tulips, and daffodils bloom along the city streets.

The W. P. Snyder Jr. stern-wheeler is moored along the Muskingum River at the Ohio River Museum in Marietta.

More Revolutionary War officers are buried at Mound Cemetery in Marietta than anywhere else in America. The cemetery is named for the American Indian mound shown in the background.

BELOW: *The Castle, a fine example of Gothic Revival architecture, was built in 1855 for Marietta lawyer Melvin Clarke. Major features of the building include an octagonal tower, a trefoil attic window, and stone-capped spires.*

The oil well was a disappointment to drillers in 1814 who hoped to find salt brine instead; they burned the oil in lamps. The Hune Covered Bridge was built in 1879 to allow better access over the Little Muskingum; it received rehabilitation in 1998.

Another feature along this route is the Mail Pouch Tobacco barns. On returning home from World War II, Harley Warrick got a job painting the Mail Pouch Tobacco logo on barns. The base pay was $28 a week, but a production incentive promised one and a half cents for every square foot covered, so Warrick decided that painting barns quickly would be the key to his success in the business. He painted two to three barns a day, six days a week. Warrick painted barns for fifty years and helped train barn painter Scott Hagan, who in 2003 painted the state's eighty-eight Ohio bicentennial barns (there's one in each county). Many of the Mail Pouch barns are black instead of red, because a black barn took fewer coats of paint. Warrick developed a number of techniques during his fifty-year career. In cold weather, he'd add a bit of paint thinner and some Seagram's so that the paint would work. Quite the character, Warrick was rumored to earn more than a few free meals from naysayers along the route, who'd bet against his ability to paint a barn in record time.

The road leads out of the Wayne National Forest and into the bucolic river town of Marietta. There's a great deal of history to explore in this town, beginning with its centerpiece, the Lafayette Hotel. Named in honor of the French hero of the American Revolution, the Marquis de Lafayette, the Lafayette Hotel was built in 1918 after a hotel fire destroyed the Bellevue Hotel, which had stood on the same spot. The town loves its history and celebrates Lafayette as Marietta's "first tourist." Throughout the hotel, you can see old oddities such as the hotel's original call-bell system, a pilot wheel from a steamboat, and two marks indicating floodwater levels from the 1936 and 1937 floods, which still impact the local psyche.

Stroll downtown to Putnam Landing, the site that commemorates the landing of forty-eight pioneers, headed by General Rufus Putnam, and see many more historical markers throughout downtown Marietta. Also downtown, the Marietta Castle is an architectural treasure. The Gothic Revival structure, built in 1859, is open for tours from June through August.

The Lafayette Hotel is a good launching point from which to explore the historic attractions in and around Marietta. The three main buildings that make up the Ohio River Museum explore three facets of river life: its natural history, the steamboat, and man's relationship with the river. The *W. P. Snyder Jr.*, the last steam-powered stern-wheeled towboat in the United States, is open for tours.

Before the days of the stern-wheeler, the first settlement in the Northwest Territory was established here in Marietta. Settlers built Campus Martius as a fort and a base of operations from which to create the now-historic city of Marietta. Though Campus Martius provides an interesting exhibition of the fort, it also explores migration in the Ohio Valley, giving this museum another layer of attraction.

Marietta is also home to earthworks that cover ninety-five acres on two high terraces. These prehistoric embankments were among the first in America to be formally protected and preserved. Historical documents show that as early as the late 1780s, resolutions were passed to protect the sanctity of the mounds. Four mound sites can be found in and around Marietta.

OHIO RIVER TOWNS
SOUTHEASTERN LEISURE AND HOSPITALITY

In southeastern Ohio, some of the state's most charming, character-filled river towns welcome visitors willing to make the drive; the big towns in Ohio and West Virginia are a long way from this remote corner of the state, so those who make the journey get a special welcome. Begin your tour with a visit to the Chester Academy inland, then hit river town after river town as you head south along the Ohio River. A wealth of restored architecture and resurrected history on Blennerhassett Island is augmented by the evidence of old money you'll find along the way to a prosperous new business: the lively Bob Evans Farm in Rio Grande.

Begin at a bend in the Ohio River to visit its biggest island. From May through October, Blennerhassett Island Historical State Park welcomes visitors with a stern-wheeler ride. It takes about three hours to really enjoy the island experience. Horse-drawn wagon rides, bike rides, and nature walks enhance a visit to the island's main point of interest, the Blennerhassett Mansion. Built by Irish aristocrat Harman Blennerhassett, the mansion mimics the architecture of Mount Vernon. With 17,000 square feet of space, the interior originally featured marvelous craftsmanship, from plasterwork to silver hardware that suspended alabaster lamps. Unfortunately, the enterprising Irishman was caught in a scandal—he was accused, along with former vice president Aaron Burr, of treason—and he fled the island, leaving his home behind. The house burned down in 1811.

In the 1970s, archeologists found the mansion's original foundation and began the painstaking process of rebuilding the home to reflect its original state of grandeur. Visitors can tour a museum on the mainland that serves as an initiation center, and then take a boat ride to the island.

Meigs County's first trial in its new courthouse took place in 1823. The first courthouse in Ohio, the building still stands on a hill overlooking the town that was governed under its roof. Chester Academy stands next door. Both buildings have been maintained over the years, housing everything from Grand Army of the Republic meetings to Daughters of the American Revolution chapters to the Ohio State Harmonica Championships. The courthouse also serves as the Appalachian Heritage Center. Programming at the center celebrates the history of the region throughout the year, but the Chester-Shade Days, the town's biggest festival in July, mark its high season.

Compare the humble original Meigs County Courthouse to the current county seat building in Pomeroy. Stately, majestic, and authoritative, the modern three-story building stands next to a cliff and offers a "ground-level"

ROUTE 21

Begin this tour at the Blennerhassett Island State Park Visitor Center in Parkersburg, West Virginia. Cross the river into Ohio using U.S. Route 50/State Route 7 toward Pomeroy— or take the long route, State Route 124, which hugs the Ohio River all the way to Pomeroy but adds miles to the trip. Forked Run State Park is accessible from Route 124. In Pomeroy, turn left onto State Route 833 and follow Route 7 south all the way to Gallipolis. (Detour on State Route 588 north to Bob Evans Farm.) Continue on Route 7 south to State Route 52 west into Ironton.

The Vesuvius Iron Furnace was built in 1833 near Ironton in Lawrence County; it operated until 1906.

RIGHT PAGE: The Chester Academy in Meigs County was built from 1839 to 1840. Next to it is Ohio's oldest courthouse, built in the 1820s.

Though it was only used as a courthouse for nineteen years, the old Meigs County Courthouse still serves as a place to court; it's used for social events these days.

entrance on each story. But the current courthouse is just one interesting site you'll encounter in a walking tour of this city that works hard to maintain its riverfront majesty. Fifty-four mural panels illustrate the walls of the town's amphitheater. And Pomeroy is also home to the Center for the Preservation of Medicinal Herbs, which is open for tours.

The town of Gallipolis, just south of Pomeroy, was settled—at least in part—by happenstance. A group of Frenchmen arrived here in 1790 holding deeds to land they had purchased back home. They had been duped and, in their confusion and anger, petitioned anyone they could think of for help, including President George Washington, who sent workers to build log houses and block houses for the settlers, welcoming them to their new home. In 1818, a group of Welsh settlers, who were traveling to their new home of Cincinnati, docked their flatboats for an evening in Gallipolis. When they woke up to find their boats adrift in the river, the Welsh women in the group said, "That's it." They began a strong Welsch settlement, which is today celebrated at the Madog Center for Welsh Studies. It's good testimony to the beauty of Gallipolis that so many settlers who arrived here never left.

When the dogwoods bud along the Ohio River, Forked Run State Park and the adjacent Shade River State Forest explode with beauty. During the region's logging, salt-mining, and iron-making heydays, the entire forest was decimated by the logger's ax. But regrowth and preservation have brought back a healthy forest filled with trees. The Shade and Ohio rivers provide diversions to boaters, swimmers, and anglers, while the deep gorges of the parks provide a challenge for hikers to conquer.

One of the region's most successful businessmen called a farm just south of Gallipolis in Rio Grande home. In a brick farmhouse on the property—once a stagecoach stop and inn—he raised six children, and probably developed a few sausage recipes in its kitchen. Now the Bob Evans Farm gives back to the community by bringing thousands of visitors each year to the farmstead, which celebrates not only the Bob Evans company but also the crafts, music, agriculture, and food of the region. Rio Grande was the site of the first Bob Evans restaurant.

A SLIPPERY SLOPE

Ohio has its share of scenic highways and byways, but a new program sponsored by the Ohio Department of Natural Resources assures that travelers of all kinds can find a route. The Muskingum River flows from Coshocton to Marietta, where it meets the Ohio River. Now that it's designated as a "state water trail," boaters can rest assured that there are adequate maps, access to docking areas, and information about the water trail, allowing the ambitious to travel through four counties along the river's path. The trail's map points out the various historical sites along the way and helps travelers pick out appropriate docking spots.

Restaurateur and sausage-maker Bob Evans was born in this house in Rio Grande in Gallia County.

This thirty-foot windmill was built in Mount Vernon, Ohio, by James Beam from 1961 to 1971. The windmill was moved to the Bob Evans Farm and reconstructed in the early 1980s.

South of Evans's graceful farm, the city of Ironton represents the beginnings of Ohio's great wealth in industry. The heart of Hanging Rock Iron Region, Ironton's landscape is a monument to the industry that built it. On the way into town, Lake Vesuvius State Park commemorates the Vesuvius Furnace—one of the most aptly named furnaces in the region. The park features Vesuvius Dam and the historic furnace. In 2004, the lake and park opened following a face-lift that necessitated the draining of the lake and brought new pathways and added opportunity for recreation to the area.

Ironton's prosperity once depended on furnaces like Vesuvius, and the city tells the story of the industry. From the humble houses where the iron workers lived, to the grand houses occupied by their bosses, to the bridges, riverports, and train tracks that lead out of town toward Rust Belt destinations that used the iron produced here, Ironton is a wonderfully urban manufacturing center in the midst of deeply wooded countryside.

SUGGESTED READING

Adams, Ian. *Our Ohio*. Stillwater, MN: Voyageur Press, 2004.

Adams, Ian, and Stephen Ostrander. *Ohio: A Bicentennial Portrait*. San Mateo, CA: Browntrout Publishers, 2002.

Baskin, John, and Michael O'Bryant, eds. *The Ohio Almanac: An Encyclopedia of Indispensable Information about the Buckeye Universe*. Wilmington, OH: Orange Frazer Press, 2004.

Kline, David. *Great Possessions: An Amish Farmer's Journal*. Wooster, OH: Wooster Book Company, 2001.

Ohio Atlas and Gazetteer. Freeport, MN: Delorme Mapping Company, 2001.

Ramey, Ralph. *50 Hikes in Ohio: Day Hikes and Backpacks throughout the Buckeye State*. Woodstock, VT: Backcountry Guides, 1997.

Vonada, Damaine. *Amazing Ohio*. Wilmington, OH: Orange Frazer Press, 1989.

Zimmerman, George and Carol. *Ohio off the Beaten Path*. Old Saybrook, CT: Globe Pequot Press, 2004.

Zurcher, Neil. *Neil Zurcher's Favorite One Tank Trips*. Cleveland, OH: Gray & Co., 2000.

The John Johnston Farmhouse was built in the 1820s and is now the main structure at the Piqua Historical Area in Miami County. John Johnston served as an Indian Agent for western Ohio from 1818 to 1829.

RIGHT PAGE: *Blue Hen Falls, near the village of Boston Mills, is a popular destination for hikers in Cuyahoga Valley National Park in northeast Ohio.*

INDEX

St. Charles Seminary at Carthagena, in Mercer County, was founded by the Missionaries of the Precious Blood. The impressive Gothic building, completed in 1922, now houses retired and active priests and brothers.

During severe winters, spectacular ice formations occur along the Lake Erie shoreline near the Marblehead Lighthouse in Ottawa County.

ABOUT THE AUTHOR AND PHOTOGRAPHER

Miriam Carey (Photograph © Billy Bass Photography)

Ian Adams (Photograph © Bridget Commisso)

MIRIAM CAREY

Miriam Carey is a writer and editor originally from Lakewood, Ohio. The author of two regional-interest books, *52 Romantic Outings in Greater Cleveland* and *365 Ways to Meet People in Cleveland*, she is also the founding editor of *Long Weekends* magazine and served as the travel editor for *Ohio* magazine. Carey began her travel-writing career at *Ohio Week* magazine and has covered the state since 1991. She thrives on discovering the dedicated and sometimes quirky people throughout the state who have the courage to champion parks projects, open small inns, and launch new tourist attractions. Carey currently makes her home in Cleveland, Ohio.

IAN ADAMS

Ian Adams is an environmental photographer, writer, and teacher based in Cuyahoga Falls, Ohio, specializing in natural, rural, historical, and garden photography. Fifteen books of his photography have been published, including *Our Ohio* (2004), and more than four thousand of his color photographs have been published in numerous calendars, posters, magazines, and other publications. Ian has conducted more than 130 seminars and workshops throughout North America on nature, garden, and digital photography. Several hundred of his Epson Ultrachrome inkjet prints are displayed in corporate and private collections.